HE HUMBLED HIMSELF

Dear Brother,
Hope you will
enjoy this book as I did.
Continue to love Jesus and
people always,

Love, Jimmy

HE
HUMBLED
HIMSELF

Recovering the Lost Art of Serving

Kenneth C. Fleming

CROSSWAY BOOKS • WESTCHESTER, ILLINOIS
A Division of Good News Publishers

Cover Illustration: Ford Maddox Brown / the Tate Gallery, London.

First printing, 1989

Printed in the United States of America

Library of Congress Catalog Card Number 88-70499

ISBN 0-89107-470-8

Unless otherwise noted, all Bible quotations are from *New American Standard Bible*, copyright © 1960, 1962, 1963, 1968, 1971 by the Lockman Foundation, La Habra, CA.

This book is affectionately
dedicated to my wife, Helena, who
has been a unique example of the
excellence of serving on the mission
field, in the home, and in the
local church.

Table of Contents

Make me a captive, Lord, and then I shall be free,
Force me to render up my sword, and I shall conqueror be,
I sink in life's alarms, when by myself I stand,
Imprison me within Thine arms, and strong shall be my hand.

My heart is weak and poor, until it master find,
It has no spring of action sure, it varies with the wind,
It cannot freely move, till Thou hast wrought its chain,
Enslave it with Thy matchless love, and deathless it shall reign.

My power is faint and low, till I have learned to serve,
It wants the needed fire to glow, it wants the breeze to nerve,
It cannot drive the world until itself be driven,
Its flag can only be unfurled, when Thou shalt breathe from Heaven.

My will is not my own, till Thou hast made it Thine,
If it would reach a monarch's throne, it must its crown resign.
It only stands unbent, amid the clashing strife
When on Thy bosom it has leant, and found in Thee its life.

(George Matheson)

Preface

Surveyed as to their personal goals in 1986, the incoming Harvard class responded: money, power, and reputation, in that order. No doubt the survey reflected the general thinking of a majority of university students in North America.

This book is also about goals, but very different from those of the average college student. The Lord Jesus made it clear that goals in the Kingdom of God are opposed to goals in the secular world. Greatness in God's Kingdom is measured in terms of servanthood, and Jesus Himself was the example: "For even the Son of Man did not come to be served, but to serve" (Mark 10:45).

Serving is a major emphasis in the Bible. *Strong's Concordance* has over 1,400 references listing *serve* in its various forms. It is obvious that the people God uses most are those who are most willing to be servants. Serving is a lifestyle, an attitude, a relationship. The pages that follow contain a fairly comprehensive study of servanthood as seen in the Bible. It is my earnest prayer that readers may learn more about Biblical servanthood, and that they will excel in imitating the perfect Servant.

Kenneth C. Fleming
Dubuque, Iowa

PART ONE

MEANING

ONE

The Lost Art of Serving

In the marketplace and elsewhere, our generation has witnessed an alarming decline in service. Old-timers remember when a service station was a place where your car was actually serviced: oil and tires were checked; windshields were washed while the gas was being pumped into the car; the employee literally ran to bring back your change while you sat in the car. Whether your collar was white or blue, you received service with a smile. Today you are fortunate to get a smile from a person who does nothing but take your money after you have pumped your own gas and done anything else you wanted done to your car.

The old idea of service was that you did something for another person to help him. Nowadays, in our era of self-service, the focus is on Number One. In the self-serve supermarkets, drugstores, and department stores all across our suburbs, it is hard to find someone who knows the product or can explain its qualities. Service is a fading concept unless it is self-service that you mean: find it yourself, put it together yourself, load it yourself.

Even in the church the idea of helping others is losing ground. On Sunday morning we go to a "service" where we sit in a comfortable pew and enjoy a good selection of music, prayers, and preaching in friendly surroundings. The better we feel about ourselves after an hour or so, the better we think the "service" was. Only a small minority do more than sit and listen. Some feel that they have "served God" by being there, but really we have been served by the preacher or teacher. In contrast, the Lord Jesus came not to be served but to serve (Mark 10:45).

The leading figure in the church is called a "minister," an old word meaning servant, though today sometimes there is not much evidence of that. Fine robes adorn many ministers who stand behind expensive pulpits on plush carpets. Many are better teachers than pastors; better at raising funds than restoring souls; better at socializing than shepherding. The head minister of a large congregation may have a job description that is far removed from the "ministry" of the Lord Jesus. He is expected to be an eloquent preacher, superorganizer, and master negotiator. He should live in a home that fits his status. His car, clothes, and golf clubs must be the best. We in the congregation want him to reflect our own lifestyle. We happily donate money to support him, but are reluctant to give our time or strength to work with him as fellow-servants. Could we be guilty of wanting him to reflect our materialistic ideals rather than to lead us as servants in the work of God?

Service is an overflow of a Christian's life to others, just as worship is the overflow of a Christian's life to God. Both start with God Himself. When we worship, we respond to God because of who He is and what He does. We are overwhelmed with the realization of His worth and work. Worship, then, is the grateful expression of our praise as we consider His glories. It may be in song; it may be in prayer; it may be in humble silence as we bow before Him. It is the vertical response of man to God.

Overwhelmed with God's love, overwhelmed with the redemptive act which transferred us from the kingdom of darkness to the Kingdom of His beloved Son, we express our love by reaching out horizontally to others (Col. 1:13, 14). "We love, because He first loved us" (1 John 4:19). Service is willing and grateful obedience to God expressed in loving acts to people. Paul urged the Philippians: "Look out . . . for the interests of others. Have this attitude in yourselves which was also in Christ Jesus, who . . . taking the form of a bond-servant . . . humbled Himself by becoming obedient to the point of death" (2:4-8). Christ Jesus, a servant, suffered for our benefit by obedience to the point of death on the cross.

Two Dimensions

The New Testament concept of a servant has two facets: acting on behalf of others, and submitting to a master. The first is represented by the Greek word *diakonos*, used many times throughout the New Testament. Most often translated "servant" in the *New American Standard Bible*, it is also translated "minister" and "deacon" (See 2 Cor. 6:4; Col. 1:25; 1 Tim. 3:12). The emphasis is on serving as an action, doing something for somebody.

The other dimension of submission is represented by the Greek word *doulos*, used even more frequently to describe the people of God. It is translated by the English word "slave" or "bond-servant" in the *New American Standard Bible* (Phil. 1:1; Eph. 6:6; 1 Pet. 2:16). *Doulos* emphasizes the idea of submission. Epaphras is described as a "bondslave of Jesus Christ," indicating that he was in submission to the complete authority of the Lord Jesus (Col. 4:12). To early Christians, Jesus Christ was Lord and Master, and they delighted to acknowledge their position as His slaves.

A third Greek word for minister is *litourgos*, which carries with it the idea of one on whom has been laid a special service to the state. When used of Christians, the emphasis is on the responsibility given to them by God. Paul had the work of evangelizing Gentiles laid on him and used *litourgos* to describe himself (Rom. 15:16).

Who wants to be a *doulos* or a *diakonos* or a *litourgos*? Very few. To be a bondslave is not a popular idea. Who wants to look up to everyone else? Who wants to carry someone else's suitcase or wash their socks? Who wants to be counted as nothing even when they work hard? Who wants to have no recognition? Even the disciples were not very keen on being servants; not one of them volunteered to wash the others' feet at the Last Supper (John 13:1-11).

Why Is Serving Unpopular?

Biblical servanthood is radically opposed to the values of the world. The world offers us a sphere in which self-interests are developed, a place for pleasure and the satisfaction of the five senses. It provides opportunity to acquire material things which are so attractive to us: clothes, cars, consumer goods. The world also allows us to advance our personal authority, a chance to "get on in the world."

The New Testament word for world is *kosmos* and primarily

means order, arrangement, adornment, beauty. It is the "present condition of human affairs, in alienation from and opposition to God" (W. E. Vine). "The ruler of this world" is Satan himself (John 12:31; 14:30; 16:11), who is also called "the prince of the power of the air" (Eph. 2:2). The "air" is "that sphere in which the inhabitants of the world live and which . . . constitutes the seat of his authority" (W. E. Vine). Satan is the ruler of those who "walk according to the course of this world" (Eph. 2:2).

Christian servanthood is opposed to the values of the world system. "If anyone loves the world, the love of the Father is not in him" (1 John 2:15). The two "loves" mentioned in this verse are opposites. The "love of the world" is a lusting after what the world has to offer: personal pleasure, material possessions, self-exaltation. They are described in this passage as "the lust of the flesh and the lust of the eyes and the boastful pride of life" (1 John 2:16). The believer who loves God must reject this false value system.

John goes on to say that all that matters in the world passes away (1 John 2:16, 17). None of it is enduring. Biblical servants will not waste their energies working for the "food which perishes, but for the food which endures to eternal life" (John 6:27).

Another reason servanthood is unpopular is that it is opposed to our "rights." We have been brought to believe that rights to health, wealth, and happiness are inalienable; that is, they cannot be taken away or transferred—they are guaranteed by law. Wars are fought over rights.

The Christian, however, must learn the difference between his rights as a national citizen and his rights in the Kingdom of Heaven. In the Kingdom of Heaven he is a servant, a bondslave. What rights does a slave possess? Wages, relationships, free time, authority, choices? None of these. The bondslave has no rights at all. He depends entirely on the good graces of his master. In human terms the master may be a cruel Simon Legree and the situation intolerable. But in the Kingdom of God the Master is the gracious God Himself who treats His servants in love. He always does what is right for them and for their best good. His servants love Him and enjoy serving Him. Yet, as servants they acknowledge that He is Lord; that all the choices are His. They have no rights of their own but to please and obey Him. In doing so they are taking the place that the Lord Jesus took when He took the "form of a bond-servant" (Phil. 2:7). Mable Williamson, a missionary to China, captures this thought in the following lines.

He Had No Rights

He had no rights:

No   right to a soft bed, and a well-laid table;
No   right to a home of His own, a place where His
      own pleasure might be sought;
No   right to choose pleasant, congenial
      companions, those who could understand Him
      and sympathize with Him;
No   right to shrink away from filth and sin, to
      pull His garments closer around Him and turn
      aside to walk in cleaner paths;
No   right to be understood and appreciated; no,
      not by those upon whom He had poured out a
      double portion of His love;
No   right even never to be forsaken by His Father,
      the One who meant more than all to Him.

His only right was silently to endure shame,
      spitting, blows; to take His place as a sinner at
      the dock; to bear my sins in anguish on the
      cross.

He had no rights. And I?

A   right to the "comforts" of life? No, but a
     right to the love of God for my pillow.
A   right to physical safety? No, but a right to
     the security of being in His will.
A   right to love and sympathy from those around
     me? No, but a right to the friendship of the
     One who understands me better than I do myself.

A right to be a leader among men? No, but the
right to be led by the one to whom I have given
my all, led as is a little child, with its hand
in the hand of its father.

A right to a home, and dear ones? No, not
necessarily; but a right to dwell in the heart
of God.

A right to myself? No, but, oh, I have a right
to Christ.

All that He takes I will give;
All that He gives will I take;
He, my only right!
He, the one right before which all other rights
    fade into nothingness,
I have full right to Him;
Oh, may He have full right to me!

(*Have We No Right?*, Moody, 1957)

Society respects the powerful, not the servants. It is more likely
to honor you for what you own than for what you are. More likely
to respect your college degrees than what you know. More likely to
acknowledge the symbols of culture you display than your attitudes
and acts of genuine love.

Society looks for power and will honor it, whether evil or good.
We have to respect political clout whether we like it or not. The
wealthy use economic power for their own purposes and with it
control others. Athletes have power to influence millions; some have
used it for good and some have not. Media personalities wield
tremendous influence, and our culture pays them tribute. It seems
that our society honors power, not servanthood.

Most of us are responsible in some way to others as employees
(servants). But employees think in terms of benefits rather than in
terms of service. Wages, retirement policy, vacation time, medical
benefits, etc. are subjects for discussion, not the quality of service we
render.

The feminist movement is opposed to Biblical servanthood. The
movement has gone beyond the promotion of women's equality and

personal dignity. The battleground today is in the role that women play in the home and church and business. Where Biblical guidelines run counter to their goals, feminists are quick to discard the Scriptures. The old-fashioned roles of homemaker and mother are servant roles and are therefore unpopular. Feminists have made themselves felt in churches as more and more women take leadership and teaching positions. They justify this by a reinterpretation of 2 Timothy 2 and similar passages.

Servants constitute an endangered species. But the danger is not as modern as some think. As soon as God made order out of the universe, Satan rebelled and in his pride declared, "I will make myself like the Most High" (Isa. 14:14). Adam and Eve rebelled when they doubted God's direction and ate the forbidden fruit. Satan had said, "In the day you eat from it your eyes will be opened, and you will be like God" (Gen. 3:5). Nimrod rebelled against God and built the city of Babylon to make a name for himself (Gen. 10:10; 11:4). History is one long story of man's attempt to discard a servant role and to establish his own proud purposes. The result has been strife, revolution, and war.

Servanthood is an art. Where God's order is established, there is harmony. What is more beautiful than a home where roles are defined and harmony marks the family as these roles are played out? How attractive the church where leaders and followers are in their proper role relationships: believers in peace worshiping together and learning together of the things of God; leaders taking their own role as undershepherds (Acts 20:28), guiding and feeding the flock of God. How blessed the nation where wise rulers insist on law and order and lead their nation to prosperity and peace. Without the proper relationship of rulers and servants, there can be no harmony. When every man does that which is right in his own eyes, you end up with anarchy as in the days of the judges (Judg. 21:25). But when the order designed by God is put into practice there is harmony. Servanthood is a key factor in the Kingdom of God.

TWO

Learning to Be Ministers

Office boy—that was to be my position? A strong sensation of hurt welled up in me. I had been a missionary among Zulu people in South Africa for just over two years. Zulu language and culture had largely occupied my time, along with pulling teeth, laying bricks, and teaching Scripture lessons in the local school. I had begun preaching simple messages in Zulu and generally being a helper to our senior missionary, Mr. Edwin Gibbs. He and his wife had just left for a furlough in the United States. Thus my wife and I were the only married missionaries on the station; I felt a kind of pleasure at being left "in charge." At last I was a "real missionary."

Now at the quarterly conference, some of the Zulu leaders agreed that one of their number should assume the "position and authority" of Mr. Gibbs. Then a question arose as to the position of the new missionary—me. His position, they said, was to be "office boy." I was no longer aware of the flickering candles and the flying ants circling ever closer until they got burned. All I could think of was, "office boy." My defenses popped up. Most of *them* couldn't even read. Didn't they know the lifestyle we had left behind in America to be here? What connection could there possibly be between being an "office boy" and the work of ministry I was called to do? When the meeting was over, a few Zulu brothers talked to me outside—they too were disturbed about the announcement.

Just then my best Zulu friend, Isaac Zindela, took me aside. He was an evangelist, a warmhearted, good man. He lived with his family in a collection of mud huts on a high ridge fifteen hundred feet above the Umzimkulu River. He and I had tramped miles up and down the hot valleys on pastoral calls. He was like a father to me, correcting my Zulu grammar and giving me insights into Zulu cultural ways. He would smile with delight when I finally understood some point after he had patiently explained it several times.

When we were alone he said to me, "Don't be upset by what you heard tonight. Just remember what Jesus said to the disciples in Mark chapter ten, verse forty-five." It was a verse I knew by heart in English. But now as he quoted it deliberately and slowly in Zulu, every word made me feel like a man being pelted with stones in Bible times.

> "For even the Son of Man did not come to be served, but to serve, and to give His life a ransom for many."

Suddenly the whole picture came into focus. I had learned that verse ten years before in Seattle. Lorne Sanny of the Navigators discipled a club of high school fellows, and Scripture memory was a part of the program. Several times before that verse had caught me when I was stealing some self-esteem to satisfy my "pride habit." Now it had caught me again, red-handed.

A Minister Is a Servant

The word *minister* echoed in the canyons of my mind for days after that. I realized again that it was simply an old word meaning "to serve." Even the Son of Man had come to serve, not to be served! Why had I come? I had come to minister, to serve, just as my Savior had. Slowly the glory of the servant character of Christ began to dawn on my pride-darkened mind, and the position of "office boy" began to take on some dignity.

Mark 10:45 has been the most challenging verse in the Bible to me. As on that occasion in 1954, again and again I have been brought to my spiritual senses by its truth. Sarcastic remarks on the tip of my tongue have been stopped by it. The tendency to self-pity has been nipped in the bud. The hurt from unthankful people has literally turned into thankfulness for the privilege of serving them. The whole concept of serving as the Lord Jesus served has been life-changing.

Learning to serve is learning to be like the Lord Jesus. Service and Christlikeness are connected because He was a servant.

> ". . . Take My yoke upon you and learn from Me, for I am gentle and humble in heart."
>
> (Matt. 11:28)

This statement is a figurative way of saying, "Submit yourselves to My instruction as an ox submits to a yoke in order to serve." I have often watched oxen being yoked. The ox must bow its head very low in order to accept the yoke, an appropriate illustration for us if we take His yoke on us. The Lord Jesus, He who is "gentle and humble in heart," is our model. And His example can become an experienced reality in each of us. It is the will of God for every believer to be a servant; and the more servant-like we become, the more fulfilled we will be.

Serving Grace

It is unfortunate that in our appreciation of the life of Christ many of us miss the impact of His discipleship training program. Our emotions are stirred as we read about a dove visibly alighting on Him, a thunderous voice out of the clouds, or a mysterious disappearance from an angry mob. We identify easily with His responses to human need: a child's death, a woman's sickness, a man's blindness. We can feel His touch of power as hungry people are fed, or as a demonized man is freed while the pigs race down into the water and drown. We love it when the children run to Him. It feels good when his sharp-tongued enemies slink away.

We also respond easily to His saving work. We understand that the salvation we enjoy came from His atoning death and resurrection, saving us from a lost eternity.

But we must understand that the implications of His teaching go much further. We need to identify with His serving grace, to share a likeness to Him as Servant. "Even the Son of man [came] . . . to serve" (Mark 10:45).

Martha, like many of us, was confused about the whole concept of service. The "work" of service was not her problem. She excelled in active hospitality: "Martha welcomed Him into her home" (Luke 10:38). She was busy with all the preparations that had to be made (v. 40). But her attitude betrayed her confusion about what true serving really is. Luke tells us that she was "distracted" by all her preparations.

Her distraction was that she was concerned about the pressure of the work, rather than about the Person she was serving. She was doing all the right things, with the wrong attitude. The Lord Jesus rebuked her, saying, "Martha, Martha, you are worried and bothered about so many things; but only a few things are necessary, really only one" (vv. 41, 42). The one necessary thing was that she focus her attention on the object of her service. She needed serving grace.

It was not the food that was important. It was not the fact that her sister's help would have hurried up the preparations. The important thing was that the Master be served by both of them. Mary was pleasing Him as she sat at His feet and listened. Martha could equally please Him by working in the kitchen. Not the activity but the attitude is the key. Martha needed grace in serving her Lord.

Serving Is Part of Discipleship

The basic demands of discipleship are easy to understand because they are simple, but are hard to practice because they are demanding. The discipleship program of our Lord includes:

(1) Complete submission to His Lordship.
(2) Complete servanthood to His people.
(3) Complete separation from the world system.

These are essential ingredients of practical discipleship.

"No one of you can be My disciple who does not give up all his own possessions." (Luke 14:33)

"Whoever wishes to become great among you shall be your servant." (Matt. 20:26)

"I chose you out of the world, therefore the world hates you."
(John 15:19)

Note that servanthood is central to living life in the Biblical
mold. The trouble is, it becomes uncomfortable for us who have
been so conformed to the world's mind-set. So we react and resist.

Me a Servant? Horrors!

Me a servant? Such a calling sounds at first like a prison sentence or
a nightmare. We associate the word with donkey work, poor pay,
lower-class labor. In South Africa the idea of servant brings up the
idea of a black man or woman working in the kitchen of a white
person. Such servants work long hours for very little reward. Sometimes they are treated well, sometimes not. This whole cultural
pattern is changing now, but it still represents the image of a servant
in that country.

North Americans too are turned off by the servant concept.
There would be no rush to answer an advertisement which read:

Servant wanted; willing, responsible, obedient and humble. Five
years experience and references required.

Americans dream of success, security, independence, rights, and
prosperity, but not servanthood. If you want to "win friends and
influence people," humble service is not the recommended way. If
you want to see your name listed in Who's Who, few would advise
you to do what the Lord Jesus taught. But if you study your Bible
and want to follow the clear teachings of the Master, serving is at the
top of the list.

True servanthood really does win friends and influence people.
It produces results beyond our dreams, though not in terms of
material prosperity. Our country is filled with successful but unhappy
people. Personal happiness has eluded them because their goals stop
at self. They have not learned that real happiness is the result of

giving, not getting—serving, not self-serving. The goals of authentic service stretch beyond ourselves and reach to others and to God. And in the process we will win friends and influence people in the same way Jesus did.

The Joy of Serving

Think of the most fulfilled people you know. You will discover that they know the joy of reaching out to others. The secret of happiness is serving.

Many find this difficult to believe because it is so contrary to the ideals of our culture. It was the same in Jesus' day. He said:

> "For whoever wishes to save his life shall lose it, but whoever loses his life for My sake, he is the one who will save it." (Luke 9:24)

To lose your life is to put aside the selfish goals of the world. This is loss only from the world's point of view. To save your life is to find spiritual fulfillment. Servants "save" their lives.

An outstanding example of a person who lost her life to save it was Helen Flint, the wife of a Bible college teacher. She used her life to serve the students. Her home was near the college, and she was always prepared to "minister" to the needs of those who came. They came by the dozens. On Saturday they came for a breakfast of waffles. Almost any day they came to use her kitchen for baking, though few left it the way they found it. Helen cleaned it cheerfully. Every student in the college was included in one of her birthday parties held every month.

Hardly a day ever passed without some student taking advantage of an open home, an open ear, and an open heart. Helen shared their joys as well as their disappointments. She gave motherly and godly counsel. Often tired, she was always smiling. Few would serve to the extent that Helen served; and few know the deep satisfying joy that Helen has. She and her husband have retired now, but she leaves a monumental testimony to the joy of service. She made hundreds happy and in the process became the happiest of all. You can do this too.

PART TWO
MODEL

THREE

Jesus Christ, Bond-Servant of God

To properly understand the Biblical teaching on servanthood, it is necessary to know the customs and laws of the Hebrews, and then to relate these to Jesus Christ as Servant. The law of the Hebrew servant is twice explained in Scripture (Exod. 21:1-6; Deut. 15:12-18).

In the agrarian economy of the Hebrews, small landowners were sometimes forced into bankruptcy. Concern for his family might lead such a person to offer himself as the bond-servant of another farmer. This was not to be a permanent arrangement, but only for six years. On the seventh he was to be released. He could not take with him wife and children acquired during his slavery; the wife must finish her contract. But he was sent away liberally provided with goods so as to make a new start possible. This provision of help was to be in proportion to how much the Lord had blessed the richer farmer, who was to remember that God had delivered him from the bondage of Egypt; thus he could happily set free the man who had fallen on hard times.

But foundational to Biblical teaching on servanthood, the slave sometimes chose not to leave his master. Perhaps he realized that for him things were better in bond-service than they were in freedom: good shelter, food, a happy home, a kind master. So he elected to stay a bondslave rather than accept his freedom.

To make this perpetual servanthood official, there was a little ceremony prescribed for the occasion. The master was to bring the bondslave to God—i.e., to the local judge who acted in God's name. The slave would publicly state, "I love my master, my wife and my children; I will not go out as a free man" (Exod. 21:5). Then he was brought to the wooden door, and the lobe of his ear was pierced with an awl, leaving a permanent scar, a mark of his perpetual servanthood. Now there was no turning back; he would serve his master for the rest of his life.

Four things characterized his service from then on. It was based on *love*, for he perceived the master's love and responded to it. "I love my master," he said. It was *voluntary*. He had an opportunity for freedom and chose servanthood instead. It was *perpetual*. There was no future way out. The master-bondslave relationship would never change. It was *total*. He was committed to do the will of the master in every respect.

Psalm 40 connects the law of the Hebrew servant with the Lord Jesus. This psalm is one of the Messianic psalms, which means it contains a reference to the Messiah which is directly quoted in the New Testament.

David was writing out of one of his experiences of rejection, probably when his son Absolom rebelled and stole the hearts of the people. Absalom had started the open revolt by a sacrificial feast. Such sacrifices, designed to point to the coming Savior who was to suffer and die for sin, had become merely ceremonial, and Absalom had abused it even further. In his rejection, David cried to the Lord in a prayer for deliverance. Remembering that he had been saved from past troubles, he trusted God for deliverance again.

The first five verses are a note of praise for previous answers to prayer. God had lifted David out of the pit and had given him a song of thanksgiving. It is in the next section (vv. 6-10) where the reference to the law of the Hebrew servant occurs. Here David declares his devotion to God as an obedient servant. He notes that God is not primarily concerned with the ceremonial side of sacrifices. "Sacrifice and meal offering Thou hast not desired" (v. 6). The legal animal sacrifices were simply pictures of the one true sacrifice for sin which was going to be offered by the Servant-Redeemer when He offered Himself on the cross.

The perfect Servant Himself speaks in the following phrase, "My ears Thou hast opened," a strange phrase until we remember the law of the Hebrew servant in Exodus 21. The Hebrew servant had his ear "opened" or pierced when he gave himself irrevocably to do the will of his master. And here in Psalm 40 the perfect Servant speaks of His ear being opened when He gave Himself to be the one true sacrifice for sin. Jehovah had made Him a servant: "My ears Thou hast opened." The sacrifice was effectual because Jehovah had initiated it.

In the next verse the Servant declares,"Then I said, 'Behold, I come; in the scroll of the book it is written of me; I delight to do Thy will, O my God; Thy Law is within my heart' " (v. 7). The Hebrew servant was to do the will of his master, and here the perfect Servant declares that he finds joy and delight in doing God's will. His service is entirely voluntary. "Behold, I come." There is more than a hint here of the Incarnation. "For I have come down from heaven, not to do My own will, but the will of Him who sent Me" (John 6:38).

The Servant of Psalm 40 is mentioned again in Hebrews, where the words of the psalm are directly applied to Christ (Heb. 10:5-7). The first four verses of this chapter state that the animal sacrifices of the Old Covenant were never able to take away sin. The repetition of them proved that. But when the Servant of Psalm 40 came into the world, He did not come with animal sacrifices but with a body prepared for the one effectual sacrifice (Heb. 10:5). His body was offered for sin on the cross.

Note that the author of Hebrews used the language of the "prepared body" in place of the "opened [or pierced] ear" of Psalm 40. But the two expressions are really equivalent, for the pierced ear refers to the servant who gave himself wholly to the master. This included his body, which in Christ's case was to be used as a sacrifice. When believers meet to celebrate the Lord's Supper, they partake of the bread which is described as "My body, which is for you" (1 Cor. 11:24).

The law of the Hebrew servant was, then, first a civil matter for the regulation of Hebrew society. Then it became part of a Messianic promise in the fortieth psalm. Finally the full truth was explained in the offering of Christ's body as the sacrifice for sin. God's Word is marvelous.

Like the Hebrew servant of Old Testament times, we have been saved by our Master from bankruptcy and failure. We too have been recipients of His grace. We have come to love and appreciate Him. He has indeed made us free to choose. But if our love be genuine, we will want only the freedom to do His will and to be His servants. The truth is, choosing to go our own way is the worst bondage, and choosing to be His servants is the greatest freedom.

Like the Hebrew servant of Bible times, we are to come to our Lord saying, "I love my Master, I will not go free, I will serve Him forever." We are to have our ear pierced as a mark of lifelong commitment to Him. The ear speaks of our ability to listen to His voice and therefore to obey Him. Consider the answer of Samuel when the Lord spoke to him as a young boy: "Speak, for Thy servant is listening" (1 Sam. 3:10). In the Zulu language of Africa the word for listen, *lalela*, is also the word for obey. Handley Moule captures this whole concept very well in his hymn of consecration:

My glorious Victor, Prince Divine,
Clasp these surrendered hands in Thine,
At length my will is all Thine own,
Glad vassal of a Savior's throne.

My Master, lead me to Thy door,
Pierce this now willing ear once more,
Thy bonds are freedom, let me stay
With Thee to toil, endure, obey.

Yes, ear and hand and thought and will,
Use all in Thy dear slavery still,
Self's weary liberties I cast
Beneath Thy feet; there keep them fast.

Tread them still down and then I know
These hands shall with Thy gifts o'er flow
And pierced ears shall hear the tone
Which tells me Thou and I are one.

The Servant's Attitude

The Old Testament type of Christ the Servant was fulfilled in His actual life and work. One of the most wonderful passages in all of Scripture on this subject is Philippians 2:3-8, a glorious unfolding of the self-humbling of our Savior. Couched within it are some of the most profound truths of His Deity and humanity ever set out.

Paul's intention in expressing these truths was not primarily theological but practical. He was urging the Philippian believers to renounce selfishness and look on others as being more important than themselves. This does not mean that the pilot will let the stewardess land the Boeing 767. It does mean that the pilot will consider her well-being and comfort even more than his own. All people have dignity as people and are to be considered important, whatever their role.

Paul goes on to urge believers to concentrate on the interests of others and not just their own personal concerns. Most of us fail here because we are so self-centered. To drive his point home, Paul urges us to have the attitude of Christ who did not hang on to His own interests, but instead concentrated on the needs of others. Putting aside His name, His throne, His dignity, His glory, and His crown, He set out to rescue us from our sinfulness, hopelessness, and condemnation. In His consideration of our desperate condition He displayed the ultimate attitude of service. Consider carefully the words of Scripture:

Do not merely look out for your own personal interests, but also for the interests of others.
Have this attitude in yourselves which was also in Christ Jesus, who, although He existed in the form of God, did not regard equality with God a thing to be grasped, but emptied Himself, taking the form of a bond-servant, and being made in the likeness of men. And being found in appearance as a man, He

humbled Himself by becoming obedient to the point of death, even death on a cross. (Phil. 2:4-8)

The emphasis here is that we should have the same attitude Christ had and that this should result in our giving ourselves for others as He did. The temptation is to accept the sacrificial offering of Himself for our sins, but to reject that same sacrificial offering as the model for living. Yet, it is preposterous to accept the one and reject the other. Having freely received the benefits of His servanthood for us, we ought to naturally respond by following His example.

The effect of studying the six steps of Christ's humiliation is that we should want, above all things, to be like Jesus. We are not looking here at the theological grandeur of these statements, but at their practical impact on our servanthood. The path Christ took begins with the glory of Deity and ends with the humiliation of crucifixion.

His Attitude Toward His Personal Dignity

"Although He existed in the form of God, He did not regard equality with God a thing to be grasped" (v. 6). The word "form" here indicates more than shape or apparent likeness. It indicates that to Christ belonged the nature and essence of God. And yet He did not consider this an advantage to be exploited or a dignity to be grasped. He was willing to put aside His outward glory.

In contrast, we sometimes consider certain acts as "beneath our dignity." As a college teacher I might, for instance, consider it below me to mop up coffee stains in the hallway. It might suit someone in the custodial department, or a student doing "slave labor," but hardly me! But considering the example of my Servant-Savior, I am to have an attitude like His, not considering my personal status a prize to be treasured or recognized.

His Renunciation of Personal Dignity

One of the most profound statements of Scripture is this: He "emptied Himself" (v. 7). Christ now goes a step further in His humiliation by making Himself "nothing" (NIV), or of "no reputation" (KJV). He waived the right of the expression of His Deity. He deliberately veiled

His majesty and power while on earth as the incarnate Son, Peter, James, and John being the only ones to see Him in His glory (on the Mount of Transfiguration). As servant He deliberately hid the outward aspects of His Deity. When they called Him simply the carpenter or the teacher, He did not correct them, much less impress them with a display of omnipotent power.

We, on the other hand, frequently let people know "who we are." We are somebody, and yet try to appear to be humble about it. So we slip in an indicator of the dignity we think we deserve. Not so our perfect Servant. He would teach us to have a heart like His, to be concerned with doing the work rather than displaying the dignity. He actually hid from view the glory of His Deity.

It sometimes happens that we enjoy a time of fellowship with another Christian and later are delighted to find that he or she is a person of some renown which had not been revealed in the conversation. That is a mark of servanthood.

His Taking the Role of a Bond-servant

Christ not only emptied Himself but took "the form [essential nature] of a bond-servant" (v. 7). That is, the Lord Jesus took the place of a bond-servant in relation to God. He was committed to do His will to the utmost degree. The Father's pleasure was His command.

This is the attitude that we are to have, the attitude of Christ who took a position of total subjection to the will of His Father. And now we are to exercise total commitment to Christ's Lordship, to step up to the door to have our ear pierced, to present our body as a living sacrifice (Rom. 12:1).

> While the warm blood is pulsing through these veins
> And health and strength and energy are mine,
> And every throbbing spring of life remains,
> This body I "present," O God, 'tis Thine.
>
> (William Blane)

His Becoming Man

The fourth step downward in the self-humbling of the Lord Jesus was that He became man. The theologians call this His Incarnation.

He stepped out of eternity and into time. He became truly man. He was made, for a little while, lower than the angels. What condescension! Milton put it into poetry:

> That glorious Form, that Light insufferable . . .
> He laid aside and here with us to be,
>   Forsook the courts of everlasting day,
> And chose with us a darksome house of mortal clay.

His identification with man in order to become their Redeemer, unique in all the history of the universe, gives us insight into the servant-like attitude required of His followers. This is sometimes called the incarnational approach to mission. It simply means that as the servant of God you are willing to identify yourself with another human being for his/her good.

His Self-Humbling as Man

Christ not only stepped down from Deity to humanity, He stepped down to the bottom of humanity. He was born in the manger of a cattle shed or cave. He grew up in poor circumstances in a despised town, Nazareth. He could identify with the oppressed and the disadvantaged. He knew pain, hunger and weariness, all associated with a world under the curse of sin.

Few believers know very much about a deliberate choice to be among those who are the despised and rejected. Yet if we would emulate the perfect Servant, we must. Too often we act in a paternal way to the less fortunate. Instead of humbling ourselves, we send a care package or a check. We salve our consciences but fail to give ourselves.

Our Lord spoke with a woman of questionable reputation at the well. He ate with publicans and sinners. He loved people as no one else has ever loved them. The Son of Man came not to be served but to serve. In doing so, He humbled Himself to be where they were.

His Obedience Unto Crucifixion

Christ's steps downward began with the glory of His Deity, but ended with the humiliation of a criminal's death on a Roman cross, the ultimate indignity. Prophetically he could say, "I am a worm, and not a man, a reproach of men, and despised by the people. All who see me sneer at me" (Ps. 22:6, 7). His obedience as a servant led Him to give Himself as a sacrifice for sin. Death by crucifixion was the most painful, the most degrading of all deaths; but our Savior was obedient unto death, "even death on a cross" (v. 8). He went to the uttermost in obedience to His Father.

The attitude of the Servant who went all the way to the cross is to be ours. "Have this attitude in yourselves" (v. 5). No road is too rough, no place too far, no pain too great. Obedience goes all the way or it is not obedience at all. In the Old Testament the Hebrew servant made a lifelong commitment to obedience when his ear was pierced. The Lord Jesus gave His life in obedience as a sacrifice for sin, and we are commanded to have the same attitude He had.

> May the mind of Christ my Savior
> Live in me from day to day.
> By His love and power controlling
> All I do and say.
>
> (Katie B. Wilkinson)

FOUR

The Full-Service Messiah

Learning to serve is not complicated, especially when we can learn from the greatest Teacher (and the greatest Servant) who ever lived. God teaches us about the characteristics of the perfect Servant through many means, including the lives of Old Testament saints. Moses, for example, is likened to the Lord Jesus:

> But the Israelites went through the sea on dry ground, with a wall of water on their right hand and on their left. . . . And when the Israelites saw the great power the Lord displayed against the Egyptians, the people feared the Lord and put their trust in him and in *Moses his servant.* (Exod. 14:29-31, NIV, italics mine)

> Fix your thoughts on Jesus. . . . He was faithful . . . just as *Moses was faithful as a servant* in all God's house. (Heb. 3:1-5, NIV, italics mine)

But even more significant than the Old Testament characters who prefigured Jesus the Servant were the direct prophecies, and among the prophets who spoke of him as Servant none surpasses Isaiah. The prophet Isaiah is the prince of the Old Testament prophets.

Chapters 40 through 66 of Isaiah's proclamation reach the highest point of Old Testament prophecy concerning the Messiah. These twenty-seven chapters anticipate the truth of the New Testament with its twenty-seven books. Like the New Testament, they begin with the ministry of John the Baptist and end with the glories of the new heavens and the new earth. (Compare Isaiah 40:3-8; 65:17-22 with Matthew 3:1-3; Revelation 21, 22.) The Messianic epic which unfolds between these two events reveals the glory of Messiah in His life, sufferings, and exaltation. It is no wonder that these chapters are quoted more times in the New Testament than any comparable section of the Old Testament.

The Messiah Is a Servant

It may seem strange that the greatest person who ever walked on the earth is characterized by the term "servant." And yet His servanthood is one of the major roles in which Christ is cast in the Bible. His role as Servant is central to Isaiah's theme because as Servant Jesus accomplished the work which the Father had given Him to do: to save and redeem sinful people (Mark 10:45). When it was completed He announced from the cross, "It is finished" (John 19:30). The servanthood He demonstrated was essential to His mission.

God wants us to study Christ the Servant and to follow Him as our model. He calls our attention to this with the statement, "Behold, My Servant . . ." (Isa. 42:1). Let us do so now.

Songs of the Servant

Four poetic passages in Isaiah are often referred to as the "Songs of the Servant." Each of the four songs emphasizes something unique about Christ, the incomparable Servant. Each of them also reveals other aspects of His servanthood which we must follow as we are conformed to His image (Rom. 8:29). The songs are found in the following passages:

Isaiah 42:1-7	The Character of the Servant
Isaiah 49:1-7	The Mission of the Servant
Isaiah 50:4-9	The Discipline of the Servant
Isaiah 52:13–53:12	The Suffering of the Servant

The description of the perfect Servant provided by these four lyrical passages is unmatched in all of literature. The first displays His servant character.

"Behold, My Servant, whom I uphold;
My chosen one in whom My soul delights.
I have put My Spirit upon Him;
He will bring forth justice to the nations.
He will not cry out or raise His voice,
Nor make His voice heard in the street.
A bruised reed He will not break,
And a dimly burning wick He will not extinguish;
He will faithfully bring forth justice.
He will not be disheartened or crushed,
Until He has established justice in the earth;
And the coastlands will wait expectantly for
His law."

Thus says God the Lord,
Who created the heavens and stretched them out,
Who spread out the earth and its offspring,
Who gives breath to the people on it,
And spirit to those who walk in it,
"I am the Lord, I have called you in righteousness,
I will also hold you by the hand and watch over you,
And I will appoint you as a covenant to the people,
As a light to the nations,
To open blind eyes,
To bring out prisoners from the dungeon,
And those who dwell in darkness from the prison. . . ."

(Isa. 42:1-7)

The Glory of His Character

Submission
As the song begins, Jehovah describes four aspects of the relationship between Himself and His Servant. When He calls Him "My Servant," the ownership and authority of Jehovah are made clear. Christ

was well aware of this in His life. Think how often Christ referred to "My Father," showing the Son's full submission to the Father.

Strength

The second area of relationship which Jehovah mentions is seen in the words, "Whom I uphold." The Lord Jesus was upheld or strengthened by the Father. Jesus, as Servant, said that the Father was really the One who did the work (John 14:10). In times of stress, too, Jesus sought and received strength from the Father.

In our service for the Lord we too must acknowledge that it is not the human instrument which accomplishes the work, but the divine strengthening. Paul said, "I can do all things through Him who strengthens me" (Phil. 4:13). The disciples learned that without the Lord they could do nothing (John 15:5).

Purpose

The third thing Jehovah says about His Servant is "My chosen one." The Servant was chosen for the great redemptive mission on which He was sent. "The Father has sent the Son to be the Savior of the world" (1 John 4:14). And Jesus said, "My food is to do the will of Him who sent Me" (John 4:34). Conscious that He was chosen for the task, He was triumphant in the most difficult of times, even on the cross.

As believers we too are chosen for the service we are to perform. To know that the omniscient God has selected us for this particular moment can change trial to triumph. Paul's experience in the storm illustrates this principle (Acts 27:23-25).

Well-Pleasing

Jehovah now says of His Servant, "in whom My soul delights." Jehovah rejoices in the work and character of His Servant. In the New Testament an equivalent expression is used twice by the Father concerning His beloved Son. At His baptism a voice from Heaven thundered, "This is My beloved Son, in whom I am well pleased" (Matt. 3:17). At His transfiguration the same voice from Heaven declared that God was well-pleased (Matt. 17:5). Every aspect of the service of the Son pleased the Father.

These four phrases about Christ the Servant give us a pattern for our service. First, we gladly acknowledge that we are His. The greater our sense of belonging and submission, the greater our effectiveness as servants. When Thomas confessed, "My Lord and my God," he was confessing his submission to the Savior.

Secondly, we are conscious that we are upheld by His "gracious omnipotent hand." This is why Paul prayed that the Colossian church would be "strengthened with all power, according to His glorious might, for the attaining of all steadfastness and patience" (Col. 1:11).

Like Christ the Servant, we too are "chosen." We are "created in Christ Jesus for good works" (Eph. 2:10). What dignity this gives to our service. It is an honor to serve the living God.

Lastly, we are to live to please our Lord, just as Christ delighted the Father. Paul challenged Timothy to be a Christian soldier whose desire was to please his Commander, to free himself from his own affairs, to be totally committed to making his Commander happy (2 Tim. 2:4). We gladly serve to make Him happy.

One of the success factors behind winning football teams is playing the game to please the coach. Players know that on Monday the films will be reviewed and their performance evaluated. With this in mind, the cheers or jeers of the crowd no longer distract them. What they want is a "well done" from the coach. Similarly, nothing should delight us more than pleasing our Lord.

Anointed with the Spirit

Isaiah's prophecy goes on to say in verse 1, "I have put My Spirit upon Him." The Holy Spirit's visible descent upon Jesus was accompanied by a voice from Heaven which declared that God was "well pleased" with Him (Luke 3:21, 22). This marked the beginning of His servant-work. There is an important link between pleasing the Father and being anointed with the Holy Spirit in both Isaiah 42 and Luke 3. These two always belong together. From this point on, the major events in the ministry of Jesus were linked to the enablement of the Spirit.

As servants, believers too need to be empowered by the Spirit. Without the Spirit our service is powerless and meaningless. When the disciples were commissioned, they were given the power of the Holy Spirit (Acts 1:8). So much of the activity of the church today is ineffective because it is dependent solely on human resources rather than the power of the Spirit of God. We tend to be well-equipped and well-organized but poorly energized.

Spirit-filled servants are effective because the power of God is working through them.

In the life of David there is a good illustration of the powerlessness of the church. In the Valley of Elah, where the Philistines were facing the army of Israel, Goliath was issuing his daily challenges to Israel without any takers: "I defy the ranks of Israel this day; give me a man that we may fight together" (1 Sam. 17:10). No one dared come forward, not even Saul. In verse 2 we are told that they "drew up in battle," but that was all they could do.

The church today is much like that. Well-trained and equipped, it looks like the church militant. But when it comes to the point of battle, we lack the Davids. When David came, he came with the Spirit of the Lord upon him (1 Sam. 16:13). Thus empowered, he shouted at the giant, "The battle is the Lord's and He will give you into our hands" (1 Sam. 17:47). This is the key to victory.

Justice to the Nations

Isaiah's world, like ours, was filled with injustice from the palace to the cottage. The coming Messiah-Servant, however, was at last going to bring justice to the nations (v. 1). Isaiah prophesied of a coming Kingdom in which justice would be established in all the nations of the world. That day has not yet come; justice and peace are still elusive. But the work of the Servant will ultimately result in justice and righteousness when He returns to set up His Kingdom.

And even before that day comes, there is a sense in which justice is now coming to the nations. As the Good News is preached around the world, it results in the liberation of people from sin's bondage. Every believer who is a true servant can bring this message to the lost people of the world. The Lord Jesus asked His disciples to lift up their eyes and look on the fields ready for harvest (John 4:35). The work of the harvest is the work of servants.

The Glory of His Service

Perhaps the most striking feature of Isaiah's description of the Servant of Jehovah is in verses 2 through 4. The Servant's character is seen in the kind of service He performs.

Self-Denying Service

"He will not cry out or raise His voice, nor make His voice heard in the street" (v. 2). The gist of the statement is that He would not raise His voice promoting Himself; in the performance of His service He does not seek recognition. How different this is from the world today. Few want their accomplishments to remain anonymous.

Jesus healed without ever saying who did it (Luke 23:9). His service was humble, gentle, quiet. He said, "I am gentle and humble in heart" (Matt. 11:29). Self-denying service is Christlike service.

Sadly, the evangelical world is sometimes infected with the self-promoting character of the secular world. Big names are splashed around in the Christian media, and the danger is that God's people may assume that God's greatest blessings accompany the biggest names. True, some of the best-known Christian leaders are genuinely humble, but humility is not an easy path. We must be constantly reminded that "He humbled Himself" (Phil. 2:8). We must deny ourselves if we are to serve as He served.

Others-Oriented Service

"A bruised reed He will not break" (v. 3). People are often damaged "reeds" with life scars that have left them bent and bruised. An aggressive leader might break off such a reed and throw it aside. Not so the perfect Servant. He specializes in straightening bruised reeds, helping them stand again under His patient, gentle care. Peter was a "bruised reed" when he denied the Lord. How could this man ever be a recognized leader in the early church? The answer lies in the ministry of the Servant who carefully restored Peter: "Tend My lambs" (John 21:15).

The ministry of straightening bruised reeds is desperately needed these days. Broken hearts, lives, and homes are everywhere. True servants see here a huge opportunity for ministry.

Not only would Messiah straighten bruised reeds, but He would restore smoking wicks (v. 3). The imagery is that of an ancient clay oil lamp with a wick protruding from the smaller opening. The wick in time became charred and encrusted, causing the lamp to sputter. It needed periodic cleansing and trimming if the lamp was to shine.

The sputtering wick illustrates the person whose light of testimony has become ineffective. The Servant of whom Isaiah was speaking will not quench a smoking wick, but rather restores it so it will shine again. Significantly, this very passage is quoted in Matthew 12:18-21 as the basis of the Lord's compassion for the sick and suffering. What service!

A needed ministry in the church is the restoration of sputtering lamps. Lives that once were bright and shining sometimes lose their glow. John Mark was one of these. He left Paul and Barnabas in the lurch on their first missionary journey and returned home (Acts 13:13). But later Paul could write that Mark was profitable to him for the ministry (2 Tim. 4:11). John Mark was shining again. No doubt there had been some lamp trimming ministry in between (probably by Barnabas).

Local churches have many dimly burning wicks that need care. Handicapped people, singles, divorcees, ex-convicts and other "out" groups are easily overlooked. Christ's servant will see that they get the restoring touch of caring love. Though broken reeds, they will stand again. Though smoking wicks, they will shine again.

The Glory of His Faithfulness

The next thing Isaiah says about the wonderful Servant concerns His faithful perseverance to the end: "He will not be disheartened or crushed" (v. 4). There is an interesting play on words in the third and fourth verses. The words translated "break" and "extinguish" in verse 3 are the same words translated "crushed" and "disheartened" in verse 4. The force of this is that the One who does not quench sputtering wicks is never quenched Himself. And the One who restores bruised reeds is never bruised Himself. He is never broken or quenched, though He serves those who are.

In Greek mythology the gods who supposedly did such wonderful things on earth were just as selfish and immoral as the people on earth. Not so when the true God sent His Servant. Though His enemies searched for flaws in His character, they found none. Christ the Reed stands unbruised; Christ the Light shines undimmed. What a Model for us, His servants!

One more thought from verses 3 and 4: a reed is bruised from an outside blow; a lamp wick becomes clogged from inside impurities. Both wicked men and Satan himself sought to bruise Christ; the subtle forces of mind and body were used to tempt Him from the inside. In both cases, the Scripture testifies that He was completely without sin.

Serving to the Uttermost

"He will not be disheartened or crushed until he has established justice in the earth" (v. 4). His faithfulness to the task remained steadfast until the work was complete. The Servant keeps on serving those whom the world ignores. Discouragement does not cause Him to lose heart when the people He serves stumble. Not only does He save to the uttermost—He *serves* to the uttermost.

The New Testament reminds us that the Lord can "sympathize with our weaknesses" (Heb. 4:15). He knows how weak we are; He remembers that we are dust (Ps. 103:14). Yet "His compassions never fail" (Lam. 3:22). Likewise, when we serve we are not to be discouraged, but rather to faithfully keep on until the work is finished.

It may keep us from losing heart if we remember that He went all the way to save us. He went through the Garden, the trials and denials, the mocking and the cross, the darkness and the loneliness. When the work of our salvation was accomplished, He cried, "It is finished" (John 19:30). He faithfully obeyed the Father until the work was complete. We too are to be constant in service. We admire greatness in sports, music, theater, business, etc. But few of us are willing to persevere ourselves. In society and in the church, there are too many spectators and too few performers. In serving we need many more who will strive for excellence and perfection.

Justice claims our attention in verse 4, for the third time in four verses. It is interesting that the Servant of Jehovah brings justice by the very opposite means used by the world today. Our contemporary world seeks its own idea of justice through force, terrorism, boycott, or political maneuvering. What a contrast to the Servant who pleases Jehovah in all that He does, acts humbly and gently (v. 3), and perseveres until His work is finished (v. 4). Universal justice is a goal of the Servant, and He will accomplish it.

Untold Millions

The last phrase in verse 4 is in the context of coming universal justice through the servant of Jehovah. It has not yet come, so the coast-lands still wait for His Law. The "coastlands" were the populated regions of the Mediterranean which had not yet heard of Jehovah or His Law. Many prophetic passages in the Old Testament express God's concern for these lands.

There is a false notion that the God of the Old Testament was exclusively concerned for His chosen people. Dozens of Scriptures contradict this idea. The God of the Old Testament was and is a missionary God, with concern for all peoples.

The application for us today is to disciple all nations (Matt. 28:18-20). The greater and final fulfillment is that Christ's judgment and justice will reach all people when He rules in righteousness.

The Glory of His Ministry to the World

The final stanza of this song touches on the glory of our Savior's worldwide blessing (vv. 5-7). The One who speaks in verse 5 is "Ha El," a name associated with the power of the Creator. He is the Creator of the heavens (including all astronomical space with its galaxies). He took special interest in the life-forms which He placed on Earth to display His wisdom and glory. The climax in this verse is that He took extraspecial care with the people He created, putting a capacity for eternal life in them. These were of greater value to Him than the inanimate universe or the other life-forms of Earth. Their value to Jehovah as people makes it important that His message reach them, so they will know how the Servant came to redeem the fallen creation.

Verse 6 explains the Servant's part in reaching all people, both Jews and Gentiles. Note that in this verse God speaks as Jehovah, the Covenant God. He speaks to the Servant, reminding Him of His calling and of the strength available to accomplish it. The language here is similar to that in verse 1. The Servant who was "upheld" in verse 1 is "held by the hand" in verse 6. Jehovah also watches over Him and makes Him to be "a covenant to the people." He came forth to His own people, the idea in the phrase "covenant to the people." This is also a reference to the redemptive work of the Servant accomplished at the cross.

A Light to the Nations
As Servant, Christ shines beyond His own people to the nations (the Gentiles) who live in darkness. This refers to God's worldwide program in "taking from among the Gentiles a people for His Name" (Acts 15:14). God's purpose is to save lost people from the darkness of sin.

This theme is developed in a number of places in the Bible. The old prophet Simeon referred to this very passage when he held the infant Jesus in his arms, using Isaiah's prophecy to confirm that the Light had come for all peoples, including Gentiles (Luke 2:25-35). All of us can be grateful for the Light that has come to us.

As servants seeking to follow the perfect Servant, we too have ministry which brings His light to the world. The Lord Jesus has said, "You are the light of the world" (Matt. 5:14). Too many of us who call ourselves His servants are not like John the Baptist of whom Jesus said: "He was the lamp that was burning and was shining" (John 5:35). The light of the gospel is needed in this dark world, and we are to shine as His lights.

In the beginning of the sixteenth century a man called Martin of Basel became a believer, but he was afraid to let his light shine. He wrote his confession on a piece of parchment and hid it under a stone in his chamber. One hundred years later the parchment was discovered. It read: "O most merciful Christ, I know I can only be saved by the merit of Thy blood. I acknowledge Thy suffering for me. I love Thee, I love Thee."

About the same time another Martin (Luther) found the truth of the gospel. He said: "My Lord has confessed me before man. I will not shrink from confessing Him before kings."

One Martin hid his light under a bushel. The other let his light shine and illuminated tens of thousands in northern Europe for a hundred years. Which path will we follow?

FIVE

Peace Mission of the Redeemer

The second of the Songs of the Servant is found in Isaiah 49. While the first song focused on the character of the Servant, the second portrays the *mission* of the Servant. This included bringing peace to the world through His suffering, and thus displaying the glory of Jehovah (v. 3).

The position of this song in the structure of the book of Isaiah is important. Of the twenty-seven chapters in Isaiah 40—66, there are three sections of nine chapters each (40—48, 49—57, 58—66). These sections are marked clearly by the phrase which divides them: " 'There is no peace,' says my God, 'for the wicked' " (48:22; 57:21). Chapter 49 begins the second section, the theme of which is redemption through the suffering Savior. In the introduction of this section Isaiah presents the Servant in a remarkable way:

Listen to me, O islands,
And pay attention, you peoples from afar.
The Lord called Me from the womb;
From the body of My mother He named Me.
And He has made My mouth like a sharp sword;
In the shadow of His hand He has concealed Me,
And He has also made Me a select arrow;
He has hidden Me in His quiver.
And He said to Me, "You are My Servant, Israel,

In Whom I will show My glory."
But I said, "I have toiled in vain,
I have spent My strength for nothing and vanity;
Yet surely the justice due to Me is with the Lord,
And My reward with My God."

And now says the Lord, who formed Me from the womb
  to be His Servant,
To bring Jacob back to Him, in order that Israel might be
  gathered to him
(For I am honored in the sight of the Lord,
  And My God is My strength).
He says, "It is too small a thing that You should be My
  Servant
To raise up the tribes of Jacob, and to restore the preserved
  ones of Israel;
I will also make You a light of the nations
So that My salvation may reach to the end of the earth."

Thus says the Lord, the Redeemer of Israel, and its Holy
  One,
To the despised One,
To the One abhorred by the nation,
To the Servant of rulers,
"Kings shall see and arise.
Princes shall also bow down;
Because of the Lord who is faithful, the Holy One of Israel
  who has chosen You."

The Servant Himself speaks, calling on the coastlands inhabited by the Gentiles to listen to what He has to say (v. 1). Probably this very passage was used by the risen Lord as He walked to Emmaus with the two disciples (Luke 24:13-35). He pointedly reminded them of what the prophets had foretold "concerning Himself." He said, "Was it not necessary for the Christ to suffer these things and to enter into His glory?" (Luke 24:26). Small wonder that their hearts burned within them while He opened the Scriptures. Isaiah 42 would have helped the disciples recognize Him; Isaiah 49 would reveal His glory.

There is a distinct similarity between the song in chapter 42 and the one here in chapter 49. It is as if they were the first and second verses of the same hymn. The Servant's calling, His being set apart, His divine preparation and protection—all these are in both of the songs.

The seven verses at the beginning of chapter 49 are a kind of conversation between the Servant and Jehovah. When the Servant speaks, He tells what Jehovah has done (vv. 1, 2, 4, 5b). Like any faithful servant, His boast is in the character and accomplishments of the Master. When Jehovah speaks, He reminds the Servant of His grand purposes and how the Servant is to be involved in them (vv. 3, 5a, 6, 7).

The Servant's Readiness for Jehovah's Work (vv. 1, 2)

After calling on the coastlands (the Gentile world) to listen, Jehovah's Servant speaks of His calling from the womb of His mother: "The Lord called Me from the womb." The Old Testament says nothing of the earthly father of the Lord Jesus, but often speaks of His mother (Gen. 3:15; Ps. 22:9, 10; Mic. 5:1-3). The reference to His mother points up a privilege of Christian womanhood: to give birth to God's nobility—His servants. Chosen to give birth to the Messiah, Mary magnified the Lord. But every Christian mother can be encouraged that her children are called by the Lord to serve as He may choose.

Brides these days are urged to pursue a career even at the expense of rearing servant-sons and daughters. But more happy is the mother whose children rise up and call her blessed, and deeper her satisfaction as they are being used of the Master. If God chooses servants from their prenatal state, then surely it is a privilege beyond compare to bear them and rear them for His service.

Note one more thing. In this song the name of the Servant was chose even before He was born (v. 1). Though the name Jesus is not mentioned in the Old Testament, the fulfillment of this prophecy took place when the name Jesus was revealed to both Mary and Joseph before His birth (Luke 1:31; Matt. 1:21). The name was important, for it identified the work He was to do: "He . . . will save His people from their sins." The name Jesus means "Jehovah is salvation." It was for this service He was called.

A Sharp Sword in Jehovah's Hand

Having established the Servant's prenatal call to serve, and His name which indicated the service He was to do, the prophet speaks now of His mouth and the words He spoke: "He has made My mouth like a sharp sword" (v. 2). The Servant Jesus spoke the whole truth, which often pierced the consciences of hypocritical Pharisees. He spoke with authority (Matt. 7:29), though men were unwilling to recognize it. He spoke with power, resulting in the sick being made well and even the dead being raised. Consider the power in the word, "Lazarus, come forth" (John 11:43). Our Savior spoke with wisdom, and no one dared ask any more questions.

Mark, author of the "Gospel of the Servant," introduces the ministry of Jesus with great emphasis on His preaching: "Jesus came into Galilee, preaching the gospel of God" (Mark 1:16). For the next three years His mouth was "like a sharp sword." Truth had never been so clear, wisdom never so consistent. One who heard Him testified, "Never did a man speak the way this man speaks" (John 7:46). Some sixty years later, when John the Apostle was exiled on the Island of Patmos, the exalted Lord was revealed to Him in Heaven with "a sharp two-edged sword proceeding out of his mouth" (Rev. 1:16). Again the sword symbolized His all-searching truth. Later, near the end of the Revelation, John saw a vision of the Second Coming of Christ in glory. In the vision His name was called "The Word of God," and again a sharp sword was seen coming out of His mouth with which to judge the nations (19:13-16). Without doubt, the Servant Isaiah saw with a mouth like a sharp sword was the same Person whose words cut to the heart of His adversaries, the same whom John saw in the glory of his revelation—our Lord Jesus Christ.

Sword or Feather Duster?

The Word of God is a two-edged sword to be used by His servants today (Heb. 4:12). The advance of the church of Jesus Christ is dependent on the effective use of "the sword of the Spirit, which is the word of God" (Eph. 6:17). Both the wrath of God and the grace of God are in that sword. God uses skilled swordmen to advance into the territory of the Enemy, and our mouths are to become like sharp swords because we speak the Word of God. Sharp swords cut, and we must be prepared for a cutting ministry when the occasion demands. It is so much more pleasant to tickle with a feather duster than to pierce with a sword. The truth, however, is not a feather duster but a sword, and the faithful servant will take courage and use it.

The key to the use of the sword is in the next phrase: "In the shadow of His hand He has concealed Me" (v. 2). The power of this sword must be under the control of Jehovah's hand. The fulfillment of this in the life of the perfect Servant is clearly seen. He was careful to use the sharp sword of His speech in accordance with the will of the Father.

The imagery Isaiah uses is that of the hilt of a sword controlled by Jehovah. The language he uses states that the Servant Himself was in the hand of God. "In the shadow of His hand He has concealed *Me*." The Servant and His words are seen as one. The word is in the Servant, who is in the hand of the Father. The Lord Jesus both spoke the truth and was the truth (John 14:6). As a good swordsman uses his sword to cut, pierce, and defend without a needless stroke, so He skillfully used His tongue with both grace and truth.

Overuse of the sword is a common temptation for many of us who are naturally aggressive in the service of the Lord. How careful we should be to insure that we are "hidden in the shadow of His hand" when use of the sword becomes necessary in our ministry. We sometimes tend to hit too hard, or to twist the blade after penetration. We must remember that it is the "sword of the *Spirit*," and not our own. And let us use it only while we ourselves are held securely in the hand of the Lord.

A Polished Arrow in Jehovah's Quiver

The song continues its theme of the mission of the Servant. But the imagery changes from the controlled use of the sword to the polished arrow ready for use. As a good servant He is ready for instant service, ready to go to any place and do any work. Isaiah uses the imagery of an arrow in the quiver of a bowman. The arrow is polished, straight, and ready for use as it stands hidden in the quiver. The Servant Himself is speaking in this verse: "He has also made Me a select arrow; He has hidden Me in His quiver" (v. 2). He waits in readiness to be sent on the mission of Jehovah.

The great mission on which the Arrow was to be sent was the securing of our salvation. The aim was centered on a place called Calvary. The Arrow had been ready from the time sin entered the world. For four thousand years it had been waiting, hidden in Jehovah's quiver. "When the fullness of the time came, God sent forth His Son" (Gal. 4:4). Jehovah's Arrow was released, and the Enemy was destroyed and salvation accomplished, right on time and right on target.

We too are to be arrows in the quiver of our Master. We are to be in constant readiness, polished and straight. How long we remain in the quiver, out of sight, is up to the Bowman. John the Baptist was hidden for thirty years and then launched on a brief six-month ministry. Paul was hidden for about ten years between his conversion and his mission. The history of the church is dotted with prepared arrows, which were hidden for a time and were then shot forth by an all-wise God and found their mark.

"What Are Arrows for but to Shoot?"

Jim Elliot, one of five martyrs in Ecuador in 1956, was one of God's choice arrows. As a college student he had a burden to reach Quechua people in Ecuador who had never heard the Good News. His brother had just left for another field in South America. Jim shared his burden with his godly parents, and when they expressed some sadness at the proposed mission, he replied:

"I do not wonder that you were saddened at the word of my going to South America," he replied on August 8. "This is nothing else than what the Lord Jesus warned us of when He told the disciples that they must become so infatuated with the Kingdom and following Him, that all other allegiances must become as though they were not. And He never excluded the family tie. In fact, those loves, which we regard as closest, He told us must become as hate in comparison with our desires to uphold His cause. Grieve not then, if your sons seem to desert you, but rejoice rather, seeing the will of God done gladly. Remember how the Psalmist described children? He said that they were an heritage from the Lord, and that every man should be happy who had his quiver full of them.

And what is a quiver full of, but arrows? And WHAT ARE AR-
ROWS FOR, BUT TO SHOOT? So with the strong arms of
prayer, draw the bowstring back and let the arrows fly—all of
them straight at the Enemy's hosts."

"Give of thy sons to bear the message glorious,
Give of thy wealth to speed them on their way,
Pour out thy soul for them in prayer victorious,
And all thou spendest Jesus will repay."
                        (Elisabeth Elliot, *Shadow of the Almighty*,
                                    Harper & Row, p. 132)

The Servant's Understanding of His Mission

The Servant Song now moves forward to reveal the purpose for
which He has been made ready. Jehovah is the speaker in this section
and He begins, "You are My Servant, Israel" (v. 3). It might appear
that Jehovah is speaking to the nation Israel here, but the context
indicates clearly that a person is to be used by Jehovah in the future
of the nation (v. 5). Christ the Servant would come from the nation
Israel and ultimately accomplish work for which Israel had responsibility. That purpose is now stated.

His Mission—To Display Jehovah's Glory

The passage states: "My Servant . . . in whom I will show My glory."
Jesus' disciples, observing Him, exclaimed, "We beheld His glory as
of the only begotten from the Father, full of grace and truth" (John
1:14). What they saw was a display of the Father's glory. The Lord
Jesus Himself could truthfully express this in His great High-Priestly
prayer: "I glorified Thee on the earth, having accomplished the work
which Thou hast given Me to do" (John 17:4). Believing people saw
Him as He served, and God was glorified. Every movement, every
response was perfect; every word was pure. Even the Roman centurion who witnessed the crucifixion said, "Truly this man was the Son
of God!" (Mark 15:39).

Do All to the Glory of God

The old Catechism is right when it states that the chief end of man
is to glorify God. Nothing in the universe is more important.

"Whether, then, you eat or drink or whatever you do, do all to the glory of God" (1 Cor. 10:31). We are to glorify God in the physical use of our bodies (1 Cor. 6:20), in the use of our financial resources (2 Cor. 9:13), and in our day-to-day relationships with each other in the local church setting (Rom. 15:5, 6). Even death is an occasion to glorify God (John 21:19).

The ultimate measure of our effectiveness as servants is the degree to which we have glorified God. Not what our human boss puts in his report, not the outward success of the project, but whether or not God was glorified. The end never justifies the means if the means used failed to bring honor to God. Faithful, patient service can be more glorifying to Him than flashy displays that impress others.

George Fellingham was a fellow-missionary in South Africa working among Zulu people. A low-key church planting and printing ministry had gone on for several decades in a small town called Ermelo. Nothing spectacular appeared to have been accomplished. One day he told me that he had often been encouraged by the words of the Lord to the disciples: "And you are those who have stood by Me. . . . I am among you as the one who serves" (Luke 22:27, 28). Mr. Fellingham had learned that faithfulness in service for God's glory was the most important thing.

The Servant's Trust

Verse 4 continues the dialogue between Jehovah and the Servant. The Servant speaks: "But I said, 'I have toiled in vain, I have spent My strength for nothing and vanity; yet surely the justice due to Me is with the Lord, and My reward with My God.'" The Servant's words indicate personal discouragement and a sense of apparent failure. This sense of discouragement comes to Him within the context of Jehovah's purposing to show His glory. There were times when outward circumstances seemed to cloud that purpose. Disappointment and discouragement are echoed occasionally in the life of the Lord Jesus as recorded in the Gospels. "He came to His own, and those who were His own did not receive Him" (John 1:11). He wept over the unbelief of Jerusalem: "O Jerusalem, Jerusalem . . . How often I wanted to gather your children together . . . and you were unwilling" (Matt. 23:37). On another occasion He sensed human discouragement as one after another turned away from following Him. "Jesus therefore said to the twelve, 'You do not want to go away also, do you?' " (John 6:67).

Apparent failure dogged the steps of other servants in Scripture as well. A classic example is Elijah sitting under the juniper tree. Sure he had failed, he asked God for death (1 Kings 19:4). Graciously the angel of the Lord touched the prophet and revived him, starting him on the road to restoration.

David experienced the feeling of failure more than once. When rejected by Saul, he fled to the wilderness of Judah where he lived in hiding for years. Later, during his reign as king, he was forced into exile by his own son Absalom. But for David, the places of discouragement became places of renewed trust in God. Some of his most wonderful psalms came from these experiences of failure: "But as for me . . . I trust in the lovingkindness of God forever and ever" (Psalm 52:8). "He only is my rock and my salvation" (Psalm 62:6). Out of the disappointments of apparent failure can come deeper trust in God.

It is to this place of trust that the Servant described by Isaiah comes. Discounting the discouraging circumstances, the Servant says, "Yet surely the justice due to Me is with the Lord, and My reward with My God" (v. 4). Though visible results are not yet seen, they are in God's hands and so are sure.

My brother, Peter Fleming, was one of the five martyrs in Ecuador in 1956. Like the others, he hoped to advance the cause of Christ by reaching people who had never heard the Good News. Auca spears ended the missionaries' lives, leaving five widows and eleven fatherless children. What could you call that but failure? But what men called failure was used by God to eventually bring the Aucas to Christ. Not only that, but from apparent tragedy came a great missionary impetus in the middle years of the twentieth century. A few days before he died, Peter wrote in his journal that he was afraid, and then went on to say that God had comforted his failing heart by words from John 14: "Let not your heart be troubled." His trust was honored by God.

The Servant's Mission
In the continuing dialogue between Jehovah and His Servant, verse 5 indicates an enlarged purpose to be accomplished: "And now says

the Lord, who formed Me from the womb to be His Servant, to bring Jacob to Him, in order that Israel might be gathered to Him (for I am honored in the sight of the Lord, and My God is My strength)." The Servant is to have a future ministry of national importance: He will be used to bring back the nation from their coming exile in Babylon. That Isaiah wrote this many years before his people were taken into exile makes the prophecy the more remarkable. When Messiah came to earth, the largest part of the nation of Israel was still outside the land of Palestine. He did not regather them at that time, and He did not set up the throne of David as promised. Men may count this as failure, but His time had not yet come.

Verse 5 concludes with the Servant's word of confidence that the national purposes of Jehovah would be accomplished: "My God is My strength." God's might was the key to the Servant's accomplished mission, which would touch the whole nation.

International Outreach

But this national ministry is merely the prelude to an even greater sphere of ministry, mentioned in verse 6. Notice this progression in the scope of the Servant's mission. In the fourth verse: personal victory arising out of apparent failure. In the fifth verse: national regathering after God's judgment of the nation's sin. Now the climax is in verse 6: international blessing arising out of light to the Gentiles who are in darkness. Here the Servant's mission is to bring salvation to the entire world.

> "It is too small a thing that You should be My Servant to raise up the tribes of Jacob, and to restore the preserved ones of Israel; I will also make you a light of the nations so that My salvation may reach to the end of the earth."

The emphasis here is on the universal character of His mission. Regathering the nation of Israel from the four corners of the earth is described as a "small thing," a rhetorical way of saying that the Servant has a far greater task to perform: to bring salvation to the whole world. He is to be a "light of the nations"; He is to shine where darkness had ruled. His mission as "light" had been mentioned in the first of Isaiah's Servant Songs (42:6). In that chapter the Light was linked to bringing liberty to the captives and sight to the blind. Here in chapter 49 it is linked to the worldwide outreach of the gospel.

When the Lord Jesus was on earth, He described Himself as "the light of the world" (John 8:12). Paul the Apostle saw that Light while on the road to Damascus and immediately began to proclaim the "light of the gospel of the glory of Christ" to others, both Jews and Gentiles (2 Cor. 4:4). In Pisidian Antioch, on his first missionary journey, there came a great turning point in Paul's ministry. He had been rejected by the Jews there (Acts 13:45), and he made a point of turning deliberately to the Gentiles (v. 46), using this passage from Isaiah to confirm that salvation to the Gentiles was God's intention (v. 47).

The message of Christ the Light has been preached in the dark places of the world ever since, and it is brighter now than ever before in history. However, the ultimate light will shine when the Lord comes back in power and glory.

The Completion of the Mission

In the last section of the song Jehovah promises that His Servant's mission will be completed (vv. 7-13). His Servant will finally be the center of the nations of earth; the rulers of nations will recognize Him as the Chosen One of Jehovah, acknowledging Him to be Sovereign over all the earth. (There is a hint here that the Sovereign One is also the Suffering One. Before He is acknowledged as King, He is called the "despised One" and the "One abhorred," v. 7.)

The two themes of this section are introduced by the phrase, "Thus says the Lord" (vv. 7, 8). In verse 7, the Servant's mission results in the worship of the Gentiles. In verses 8-12 the Servant's mission brings the restoration of Israel.

Jehovah, speaking in verse 7, calls Himself both the "Redeemer" and the "Holy One" of Israel; He is Savior as well as Judge. These two names are often combined in Isaiah's prophecy (41:14; 43:14; 47:4; 48:17; 49:7; 54:5). The rejected Savior is also the ruling Judge of all the earth. The Servant who is "abhorred" by the tiny nation of

Israel will ultimately be acknowledged by the rulers of great nations as they bow in humility before Him (v. 7). This verse takes us from rejection by His people, the Jews, to recognition by Gentile kings.

The promise of Jehovah here is that Gentiles will worship Him. He who submitted to Roman rule in His first coming ("The Servant of rulers") will become King of all earthly kings in His Second Coming ("Princes shall also bow down"). God's faithfulness is seen both in the Servant's suffering and in His exaltation.

Israel's Restoration

The second theme of this section is Jehovah's promise to restore the nation Israel at the appointed time. Again the theme begins with "Thus says the Lord." Jehovah is speaking to His Servant in regard to the coming "day of salvation," the time when the work of the Servant would be accomplished. "When the fullness of the time came, God sent forth His Son" (Gal. 4:4). Paul quotes this verse from Isaiah to urge the Corinthians to believe (2 Cor. 6:2). But the more complete fulfillment of it will come in the end-times. Only then will the four promises of this section be literally fulfilled.

Four Promises to Israel

First of these promises (vv. 8-13) is that of the restored land (v. 8). The Servant is associated with covenant promises of a stabilized world when the people of Israel would again possess the land. Second is the promise of the release of captives (v. 9a). Third is the shepherding of Israel as Jehovah's flock (vv. 9b, 10). And fourth, the way back to the land is cleared of obstacles so Jehovah's people can return from all directions (vv. 11, 12). These promises are in reverse order, with the final result mentioned first. All these great covenant promises will be fulfilled through Jehovah's Servant. The grandeur of the promises underscores the privilege of the Servant in their fulfillment; true service always brings dignity.

The song ends with a doxology of praise to Jehovah. The Servant's work is completed, so all of creation is summoned to sing His praises:

Shout for joy, O heavens! And rejoice, O earth!
Break forth into joyful shouting, O mountains!
For the Lord has comforted His people,
And will have compassion on His afflicted.

(v. 13)

POLISHED, HID, WELL-PLEASING

O Lord, I would be burnish'd,
　　And in Thy quiver hid:
By Thee prepared and furnish'd,
　　To do as Thou wilt bid.
Devoted to Thy service,
　　A waiting one I'd be,
That I may be well-pleasing.
　　O Master, unto Thee.

Though trials the severest
　　May crush and wound my heart,
Though ties be snapped—the dearest—
　　As with the rust I part,
Yet *polish* me till in me
　　Thy likeness Thou shalt see,
That I may be well-pleasing,
　　O Master, unto Thee.

Then *hid* within Thy quiver
　　I near Thy hand would lie,
Content if there, though never
　　Observed by human eye:
When active I'll be happy,
　　When passive I shall be
Still happy, if well-pleasing,
　　O Master, unto Thee.

O this is what I covet—
　　Thy sweet, approving smile;

Earth's praise, if I should love it,
   Would but my heart beguile.
I know that at Thy coming
   Rich my reward shall be,
If I be found well-pleasing,
   O Master, unto Thee.

(William Blane)

SIX

Jesus Christ, Disciple

The unfolding revelation of the Servant in Isaiah opens further in the fiftieth chapter. This remarkable song contains insights into the life of Jesus as Servant that are unique in all the Old Testament.

The Servant's suffering is brought into prominence in this passage. In the first song His humiliation was not even mentioned. In the second, it was suggested in terms of being "despised" and "abhorred" (49:7). Here the sufferings of the Servant are much more evident, though the full development of this theme awaits the final song. His suffering is here seen in the context of His commitment, which is the principal theme. The Servant Himself is speaking:

> The Lord God has given Me the tongue of disciples,
> That I may know how to sustain the weary one with a word.
> He awakens Me morning by morning,
> He awakens My ear to listen as a disciple.
> The Lord God has opened My ear;
> And I was not disobedient,
> Nor did I turn back.
> I gave My back to those who strike Me,
> And My cheeks to those who pluck out the beard;
> I did not cover My face from humiliation and spitting.
> For the Lord God helps Me,

Therefore, I am not disgraced;
Therefore, I have set My face like flint,
And I know that I shall not be ashamed.
He who vindicates Me is near;
Who will contend with Me?
Let us stand up to each other;
Who has a case against Me?
Let him draw near to Me.
Behold, the Lord God helps Me;
Who is he who condemns Me?
Behold, they will all wear out like a garment;
The moth will eat them.
Who is among you that fears the Lord,
That obeys the voice of His Servant,
That walks in darkness and has no light?
Let him trust in the name of the Lord and rely on his God.
Behold, all you who kindle a fire,
Who encircle yourselves with firebrands,
Walk in the light of your fire
And among the brands you have set ablaze.
This you will have from My hand;
And you will lie down in torment.

(Isa. 50:4-11)

Commitment to Discipline

Discipline is the path to authentic servanthood. In this passage the perfect Servant speaks of His voluntary commitment to Jehovah as a disciple, one who submits to a training process to fit him for a purpose.

The Lord chose twelve men and trained them to serve God. We call them "disciples" (disciplined ones). The remarkable thing is that the Divine Person who trained these twelve disciples here identifies Himself as a "disciple" of God. This song is very instructive for us who would be disciples of the Servant.

In modern English we usually associate the word *discipline* with the idea of punishment, correction designed to teach and train. We frail humans need that form of discipline, but not so the perfect Servant who knew no sin. The discipline in view here is that training which produces desired character or ability and is voluntarily entered. Just as university students submit to authority to be trained in given areas of knowledge (disciplines), so the Servant voluntarily submitted to authority and training for a purpose.

The Controlled Path to Excellence

A key to understanding this song is in the repetition of a name for God which is not found in the other Servant Songs. It is the name "Adonai Jehovah," often translated "Lord God," indicating sovereign superiority. Four times it is used in the "Song of the Servant's Commitment" (vv. 4, 5, 7, 9).

The authority stressed in the name "Adonai Jehovah" is the basis of the Servant's submission as a disciple. To the Sovereign Lord He willingly commits Himself as He treads the pathway of discipline, the path to excellence. This applies not only to the Lord Jesus on earth, but to all who would take His yoke and learn from Him (Matt. 11:29). Several important areas of discipline are mentioned in the passage which were present in the life of Jesus.

The Disciplined Tongue

The Servant's tongue is mentioned first. He says that the Sovereign God has given Him the "tongue of disciples" (v. 4). His speech was in full subjection to the Father (John 8:28). The wording in Isaiah implies that the Servant has fully learned and has been thoroughly instructed. The words He spoke were received from His teacher.

No member of the human body is a better indicator of the quality of one's discipline than the tongue. The Lord Jesus was always in control of His speech, so much so that people marveled. They wondered "at the gracious words which were falling from His lips" (Luke 4:22). "Never did a man speak the way this man speaks" (John 7:46).

Control of His tongue did not mean He watered down the truth or gave wishy-washy answers. He was always ready to speak out for righteousness and justice, even though some were offended. Because He controlled His tongue, He never had to regret what He said. He spoke only that which was consistent with the glory of the Father and came from the Father (John 12:49).

Who Can Tame the Tongue?

The history of God's people overflows with situations where irresponsible words have caused hatred and divisions and wounds which never healed. When James says, "No one can tame the tongue" (James 3:8), he is correct.

But the good news is that what no man can do, God can. The tongue under God's control can not only be prevented from inflicting damage, but can become a channel of untold blessing to the world. Comfort, hope, life, and edification can all come from the tongue. The perfect Servant was given the "tongue of disciples" in order to "sustain the weary one with a word" (v. 4).

In his first years of discipleship Peter was often afflicted with an undisciplined tongue. For instance, he suggested building three tabernacles on the Mount of Transfiguration, indicating the Lord was on the same level as Moses and Elijah (Matt. 17:4). He suggested that suffering and death should never come to the Lord, which prompted the Savior's reply, "Get behind Me, Satan" (Matt. 16:21-23). Again, when Jesus wanted to wash his feet, Peter tried to insist that he be washed all over (John 13:9). Peter was quick to say, "I will lay down my life for You," but was brought up sharply when the Lord said to him, "A cock shall not crow, until you deny Me three times" (John 13:37, 38).

But the undisciplined tongue of Peter became the "tongue of disciples." It was Peter's tongue which expressed, "Thou art the Christ, the Son of the living God" (Matt. 16:16). It was Peter who stood up on the Day of Pentecost and preached forgiveness of sins to the Jews from fourteen nations (Acts 2:14ff.). Peter's message introduced the grace of God to the Gentiles in the home of Cornelius (Acts 10). Peter used his tongue to defend the unity of the church when many would have separated the Jewish and Gentile believers (Acts 15:7-11). The same Peter wrote in one of his letters, "Whoever speaks, let him speak, as it were, the utterances of God"; "not returning . . . insult, but giving a blessing instead" (1 Pet. 4:11; 3:9).

Many of us as God's servants today need to follow the example of the perfect Servant and to learn what Peter learned about the discipline of the tongue.

Commitment to Obedience

The next section in the "Song of the Servant's Discipline" concerns the ear of the Servant:

> He awakens me morning by morning,
> He awakens My ear to listen as a disciple.
>
> (v. 4)

There is a connection between the learned tongue and the listening ear. Many of us fail at this point, but not so the perfect Servant who is speaking. At least two things are seen here.

First, His listening was constant and consistent, "morning by morning." In the life of Jesus there are several references to His life alone with the Father. Mark 1:35 states that the Lord arose in the early morning to go to a lonely place for private prayer. Luke tells us that "He Himself [Jesus] would often slip away to the wilderness and pray" (Luke 5:16). This regular communion with His Father was a source of spiritual strength for each day.

Since that "morning by morning" listening was vital to the practical servanthood of Christ, can it be less important for us? Only as we listen do we learn. I well remember my grandfather during boyhood days. He would drop "pearls of wisdom" as he stroked his white goatee. Occasionally when he thought that we were not listening attentively enough he would quote an old English poem.

> A wise old owl sat on an oak.
> The more he heard, the less he spoke.
> The less he spoke, the more he heard.
> Why aren't you like that little bird?

All of us need to be instructed regularly by the Lord. Perhaps the most effective opportunity for this is what is sometimes called the "quiet time." This is when we take time before the Lord with an open Bible, an open mind, and an open heart. Morning communion, perhaps the best time for most people, as it was for the Lord Jesus, prepares our souls for the activities of the day. Such time with the

Master stimulates us to "walk with the Lord in the light of His Word" and equips us for spiritual battle against the flesh, the world, and the Enemy. Our effectiveness as servants of God depends on our willingness to listen as disciples.

In 1946 I was in Chonju, Korea, part of the U.S. Army occupation forces. A concrete watchtower stood on the top of the hill where my unit was stationed. There, weather permitting, I went in the early mornings for my "quiet time." A verse that challenged me then was:

> I will stand upon my watch,
> and set myself upon the tower,
> and will watch to see what he will say unto me,
> and what I shall answer when I am reproved.
> (Hab. 2:1, KJV)

Many would-be servants are slow to detect the touch of God, who longs for us to discipline ourselves to listen. And true listening leads to obedience.

The Servant says in our passage, "I was not disobedient." The faithful servant will be quick to obey every word of his master. In the Zulu language of Africa, the one word *lalela* means both to listen and to obey. When the Zulu school principal asks his students to *lalela* he is really saying, "Listen to me *and* obey me."

Commitment to Submission

The "awakened ear" of obedience is followed by the "opened ear" of submission (v. 5). This refers to a law of the Hebrews (Exod. 21:1-11; Deut. 15:12-18) under which a poor man might sell himself to serve a master for six years. In the seventh year, however, he was offered his freedom. But if he enjoyed his work and loved his master, he could voluntarily commit himself to lifelong servitude. A public declaration of this was confirmed by having his ear pierced with an awl, leaving a permanent mark on his body for all to see. He was a bond-servant for life.

As we have already seen, this "law of the Hebrew servant" is applied to the Lord Jesus in Scripture. Psalm 40, a Messianic psalm, speaks of Messiah as Jehovah's Servant, obedient unto death. Isaiah 50:4-11 is the "Song of the Servant's Commitment." And Hebrews 10 quotes Psalm 40 in reference to the Servant's delight in commitment to the will of Jehovah. The pertinent phrases in all this are:

> "If the slave plainly says, I love my master . . . I will not go out as a free man . . . his master shall pierce his ear with an awl." (Exod. 21:5, 6)

> Sacrifice and meal offering Thou hadst not desired. My ears Thou hast opened. . . . I come . . . to do Thy will, O my God. (Ps. 40:6-8)

> The Lord has opened my ear; and I was not disobedient, nor did I turn back. (Isa. 50:5)

> "Sacrifice and offering Thou hast not desired, but a body Thou hast prepared for me. . . . I have come . . . to do Thy will, O God." . . . by this will we have been sanctified through the offering of the body of Jesus Christ once and for all. (Heb. 10:5-10)

The voluntary commitment of Jesus the perfect Servant to do the will of Jehovah is clearly seen. The will of Jehovah was that He sacrifice Himself as an offering for sin, and as a committed bond-slave our Savior was obedient unto death. The mark of His commitment was illustrated by the pierced ear, but actually accomplished in His body on the cross. Thus the writer of Hebrews modified the quotation from Psalm 40, specifically referring to the body of the Lord Jesus. Thomas saw those marks and worshipfully exclaimed, "My Lord and My God!" (John 20:28).

In John's Revelation of the Lamb in Heaven ("standing as if slain"), the angels, living creatures, and elders fell down before Him and sang in worship, "Worthy is the Lamb that was slain" (Rev. 5:6, 12). He will bear those marks in His body through eternity, and we will worship Him forever with full hearts.

The model Servant never shrank from the enormity of the task He was given. "I was not disobedient, nor did I turn back" (v. 5). The

Servant never refused to fully accept or fully perform the Master's commandment. For Him there was no turning back. That is perfect obedience.

Commitment of Suffering

The Servant's submission is now taken one step further—to His suffering (v. 6). The obedient Servant must pay the price of His commitment. His lonely path leads forward to the agony of the Garden, to the mockery of the trials and the torture of the crucifixion.

The active verbs in verse 6 indicate the deliberate willingness of Jehovah's Servant to suffer. This truth is often reflected in the Gospels (e.g., John 10:18). He was not the unfortunate victim of a cruel plot, but intentionally gave Himself for us.

He "gave [His] back" to the whips of scourging (see Matt. 27:26). Such punishment was designed for criminals; the repeated lashes were horribly painful. The Servant also gave His cheeks "to those who pluck out the beard." While there is no direct reference to this in the New Testament, it is consistent with His trial before Caiaphas, the High Priest (Matt. 26:67). He never flinched during the humiliation of being blindfolded or punched in the face and then jeeringly asked who hit Him. He gave His face to that. In contemptuous fury they spat in His face as if He were the lowest of criminals (Matt. 26:67; 27:30). What a Servant! He "delivered Himself up for me" (Gal. 2:20).

There is a sense in which every faithful servant's implicit obedience usually ends in some form of suffering, just at it did for Paul and Peter and others in the New Testament record. The servant is "not greater than his master" (John 13:16), and can therefore expect suffering. This is not asceticism, but commitment to a purpose for the sake of others.

Commitment Based on Confidence

The theme of commitment continues in verses 7-9 with the declaration of Jehovah to help His Servant: "The Lord God helps me." Note that for the third time the name for Jehovah is "Lord God"— the Almighty One who answers prayer and looks after His people.

With the Almighty's help, the Servant is completely confident even in circumstances of pain and suffering (vv. 5, 6).

The word used here for "helps" was often used to denote military assistance in the Old Testament. Here, however, the context suggests not outside help (such as an infantry battalion), but more probably inward help regarding attitude of mind and determination. The idea seems to be that Jehovah will give His Servant the perseverance and patience to be perfectly obedient.

The result of the Servant's determination is that He is not disgraced. Even though the suffering will result in death, it is not a disgrace because that death is for a noble purpose. It is implied here that Jehovah will vindicate Him, and this knowledge gives His Servant fresh courage and strength for the task.

Face Like Flint

With the twofold promise that the Lord God would help Him and that He would not be disgraced, the Servant declares His determination to complete His work: "I have set my face like flint" (v. 7). In Bible times flint was used in cutting tools when iron and bronze were not available. Here it indicates the determined character displayed in the Lord Jesus as He accepted His cross. Luke used similar language to record the Lord's moving toward Jerusalem and the crucifixion (Luke 9:51). God worked in Ezekiel in the same way (Ezek. 3:8, 9). Facing a life of pressure and disappointment, there was no turning back.

Again the servant declares that He will not be put to shame (v. 7). Wicked men tried to impugn Him in mock trials and in undeserved judgment, but could not. As a Servant perfectly doing the will of His Master, He was never put to shame.

In verse 8 the Servant is cleared of all blame. His enemies said His suffering proved that Jehovah had deserted Him and that he was receiving the just due for sins committed. But Jehovah fully vindicated His Servant/Son in the Resurrection, Ascension, exaltation, and coming Kingdom (see Isa. 52:13). He is vindicated as the perfect Servant, and His enemies are proved wrong. These very words of Isaiah may have comforted Christ in the dark hours of Calvary.

The Enemies Challenged

The Servant, confident of His vindication, now challenges his adversaries: "Who will contend with Me? Let us stand up to each other; who has a case against Me? Let him draw near to Me" (v. 8). It is an unanswered challenge. No one can rightly accuse the perfect Servant. Paul climaxes his argument in Romans with a series of similar challenges (Rom. 8:33-35). The person whose righteousness is based on the risen Savior hurls out the challenge, "Who will bring a charge . . . who is the one who condemns . . . Who shall separate us from the love of Christ?" No one!

The Servant is also confident of the defeat of His enemies (v. 9). Beginning with a repetition of the fact that the Sovereign Lord helps Him and will vindicate Him, the Servant says of His enemies, "They will all wear out like a garment; the moth will eat them." These figures of speech indicate the gradual but certain destruction of the enemy. Their accusations would finally come to nothing in the court of the Judge of the Universe. Among these humiliated enemies the perfect Servant stands tall.

Application and Summary

In the last two verses of this Servant Song (vv. 10, 11), Jehovah speaks directly to two categories of people: the faithful and the unfaithful. The faithful are exhorted to trust; the unfaithful are warned that their chosen path will end in judgment.

In Jehovah's question, "Who is among you that fears the Lord, that obeys the voice of His Servant?" (v. 10), the "who" are the faithful found among the "you," the unfaithful. It is always like that in this life. The faithful are a minority who fear the Lord and obey the voice of His Servant. Since they hold Jehovah in holy reverence, they will certainly be obedient to His Servant.

Walking by Faith in the Dark

"Let him who walks in the dark, who has no light, trust in the name of the Lord and rely on his God" (v. 10b, NIV). The faithful are exhorted to "trust" in the Lord and to "rely" on God, though they are walking in darkness. They are walking by faith, not by sight; they cannot clearly see through all the outward circumstances. Like the

Servant, they sometimes walk in "the valley of the shadow of death" (Ps. 23:4). There may be times of suffering for them, as there were for the Servant of Jehovah (vv. 7-9). They are to imitate the Servant's trust when He walked in the dark, He who exclaimed, "Behold, the Lord God helps Me" (v. 9). We as servants of the Servant can learn to trust as He trusted, to rely on God as He did. The hymnwriter, using this verse from the *King James Version*, put it very well:

> Stayed upon Jehovah, hearts are fully blest,
> Finding as He promised, perfect peace and rest.

The psalmist also expressed this truth:

> The Lord is my light and my salvation;
> Whom shall I fear?
> (Ps. 27:1)

Finally Jehovah turns His attention to the unfaithful (v. 11), those who trust in themselves rather than in the Lord. They are identified as those who light fires and surround themselves with firebrands. That is, when they find themselves in darkness, they try to provide a light of their own making instead of turning to God.

The attitude of Jehovah to such unbelievers is clearly stated, because they have rejected Him and refused the word of His Servant. Thus the Lord tells them, "Walk in the light of your fire," knowing it will end in judgment:

> This you will have from My hand;
> And you will lie down in torment.
> (v. 11)

What a contrast to the faithful who find the presence of Jehovah a comfort and strength.

I'd rather walk with God in the dark than walk alone in the light.

SEVEN

Song of the Suffering Servant

In Isaiah 52:13—53:12 we find the climax of the Songs of the Servant. Polycarp, the church father from Smyrna, called this section "the golden passionale of the Old Testament." The high point in all Messianic prophecy, it speaks of Messiah's suffering and work more extensively than any other Old Testament passage. It is directly quoted in the New Testament seven times and alluded to another twelve times.

The focus of Isaiah 53 is Messiah the Servant in His suffering and glory. As we behold "My Servant" (52:13), may we be conscious that we are seeing the King of Glory in the form of a servant. And so doing, may we be changed into His likeness (2 Cor. 3:18).

> Behold, My servant will prosper,
> He will be high and lifted up, and greatly exalted.
> Just as many were astonished at you, my people,
> So His appearance was marred more than any man,
> And His form more than the sons of men,
> Thus He will sprinkle many nations,
> Kings will shut their mouths on account of Him;
> For what had not been told them they will see,
> And what they had not heard they will understand.
> Who has believed our message?

And to whom has the arm of the Lord been revealed?
For He grew up before Him like a tender shoot,
And like a root out of parched ground;
He has no stately form or majesty
That we should look upon Him.
Nor appearance that we should be attracted to Him.
He was despised and forsaken of men,
A man of sorrows, and acquainted with grief;
And like one from whom men hide their face.
He was despised, and we did not esteem Him.
Surely our griefs He Himself bore,
And our sorrows He carried;
Yet we ourselves esteemed Him stricken,
Smitten of God, and afflicted.
But He was pierced through for our transgressions,
He was crushed for our iniquities;
The chastening for our well-being fell upon Him,
And by His scourging we are healed.
All of us like sheep have gone astray,
Each of us has turned to his own way;
But the Lord has caused the iniquity of us all
To fall on Him.
He was oppressed and He was afflicted,
Yet He did not open His mouth;
Like a lamb that is led to slaughter,
And like a sheep that is silent before its shearers,
So He did not open His mouth.
By oppression and judgment He was taken away;
And as for His generation, who considered
That He was cut off out of the land of the living,
For the transgression of my people to whom the stroke was
    due?
His grave was assigned to be with wicked men,
Yet with a rich man in His death;
Although He had done no violence,
Nor was there any deceit in His mouth.
But the Lord was pleased
To crush Him, putting Him to grief;
If He would render Himself as a guilt offering,
He will see His offspring,

He will prolong His days,
And the good pleasure of the Lord will prosper in His hand.
As a result of the anguish of His soul,
He will see it and be satisfied;
By His knowledge the Righteous One,
My Servant, will justify the many,
As He will bear their iniquities.
Therefore, I will allot Him a portion with the great,
And He will divide the booty with the strong;
Because He poured out Himself to death,
And was numbered with the transgressors;
Yet He Himself bore the sin of many,
And interceded for the transgressors.

(Isa. 52:13—53:12)

There are five stanzas here, each of which covers three verses in our English Bibles and is easily recognizable. The stanzas center on the following progressive themes.

The Servant Exalted   (52:13-15)
The Servant Rejected   (53:1-3)
The Servant Wounded   (53:4-6)
The Servant in Death   (53:7-9)
The Servant Satisfied   (53:10-12)

The first and last stanzas are like mountain peaks describing the glory of the Servant. The middle three are like a valley in between, describing His suffering and death. A miniature of the same pattern is seen in the first stanza.

First Stanza: The Servant Exalted

The Prospect of Exaltation   (52:13)
The Valley of Humiliation   (52:14)
The Height of Glory   (52:15)

Jehovah begins the Song of the Servant by claiming Him as His own ("My Servant"), whose work would be completed successfully and so He would be exalted. Three phrases are used to express this in verse 13 ("raised," "lifted up," and "highly exalted," NIV), each surpassing the one before. These may be linked to the Resurrection, Ascension, and enthronement of the Servant when he had completed His work. "God highly exalted Him" (Phil. 2:9), "far above all rule and authority and power and dominion" (Eph. 1:21).

The next verse speaks of His humiliation and the utter astonishment of people as they see the intensity of His suffering. His face was disfigured beyond recognition. His body was marred so badly that He seemed inhuman.

> Death and the curse were in that cup.
> O Christ, 'twas full for Thee.
> But Thou hast drained the last dark drop.
> 'Tis empty now for me.
> Thy form was scarred, Thy visage marred.
> Now blessing draught for me.

The final verse in this first stanza takes us back to the heights of the Servant's glory. As Jews were so astonished because of His humiliation at Calvary, so Gentile nations will be astonished at the glorious exaltation of His Second Coming.

The last two phrases of verse 15 were used by Paul as a rationale to evangelize the Gentiles (Rom. 15:21). Paul had a servant's heart for people who had less opportunity to hear the gospel. May we do no less, for the day of Messiah's coming when the nations will be astounded is fast approaching.

Second Stanza: The Servant Rejected

The Rejection of the Report	(53:1)
The Pain of Rejection	(53:2)
The Reason for Rejection	(53:3)

As the Song of the Servant's Suffering moves into the second stanza, a future believing Jewish remnant speaks. Explaining how they treated Messiah the Servant at His first coming, they look on Him whom they pierced and mourn (Zech. 12:10).

The Evidence Rejected

They begin with the question, "Who has believed our message (lit. "that which we heard")?" They had heard about the glorious Servant and His humiliation. But the implication here is that almost no one believed. They had seen evidence of the "arm of the Lord" in His signs and miracles, but had rejected it. They ate the loaves and fishes, and yet refused the One who fed them. The Lord Himself told them that Isaiah's prophecy referred to their unbelief:

> But though He had performed so many signs before them, yet they were not believing in Him; that the word of Isaiah the prophet might be fulfilled, which spoke, "Lord, who has believed our report? And to whom has the arm of the Lord been revealed?" (John 12:37, 38)

The "arm of the Lord" refers to His saving power, His breaking into human affairs for the redemption of His people. The phrase is used of Israel's deliverance from bondage in Egypt at least ten times. For example:

> "I will redeem you with an outstretched arm." (Exod. 6:6)

> "And you shall remember that . . . the Lord thy God brought you out . . . by an outstretched arm." (Deut. 5:15)

That "arm" was displayed by Messiah the Servant and was refused. This refusal is further explained in verse 2.

He was rejected when He did not come in the form they expected. They expected the sudden appearance of a majestic cedar, but He came as a tender shoot growing out of a stump (Israel's kingly line, which had been cut off since the last king, Jehoichin, was deported in 597 B.C.). Isaiah (11:1) had prophesied that Messiah would come as a "shoot" from the "stem" of Jesse (David's father), but they were not looking for a tender shoot. They did not think that the baby born in Bethlehem could be their Messiah and consequently missed His fresh loveliness and moral perfection. Jehovah saw His beauty, but His own people did not.

The Servant was not only seen as a shoot, but as "a root out of parched ground" (v. 2). This is the imagery of a vineyard in winter when gnarled and ugly vine stumps are most unpromising in appearance. Israel did not guess that this was the true Vine (John 15:1).

He had no "stately form or majesty" which they supposed would mark Messiah. Joseph was "handsome in form," as was David (Gen. 39:6; 1 Sam. 16:2); but the Servant did not fit the humanistic ideals of the first century. True beauty was in Him, but they missed it.

The Sorrow and Pain of Rejection

"He was despised" (literally, "treated with contempt") (v. 3). He was treated as having no value by His own people. "He came to His own, but His own did not receive Him" (John 1:11). When many were leaving Him, Christ asked His disciples, "You do not want to go away also, do you?" (John 6:67), and even they forsook Him in the Garden (Matt. 26:56). They forsook Him at the cross too; in fact, even God the Father forsook Him there (Matt. 27:46).

The Servant is called "a man of sorrows" (v. 3). His life was one of painful endurance. He was also "acquainted with grief" (or sickness). Thus He could "sympathize with our weaknesses" (Heb. 4:15). He felt the effects of sin's ravages, though never Himself tainted by sin. He was a sorrowful and grieving man.

People's reactions to this were negative. As one turns from a repulsive object, they hid their faces. They despised Him (repeated for emphasis at the beginning and end of the verse). They concluded that He had no real importance in their lives; they "did not esteem Him."

> Man of Sorrows, what a name
> For the Son of God who came
> Ruined sinners to reclaim,
> Hallelujah, what a Savior.

Third Stanza: The Servant Wounded

The Human Occasion of His Suffering   (53:4)
The Diving Initiative of His Suffering   (53:5)
The Human Necessity of His Suffering   (53:6)

This stanza explains the previous one as converted Israel in the future understands their rejection of Messiah when He came the first time. There was an unexpected purpose in what appeared to be the greatest mistake in the history of the world. This is the force of the word "surely" with which the stanza begins.

The Human Occasion of His Suffering

Unexpectedly, it was the despised One, from whom they hid their faces, who Himself bore the punishment for our sin (v. 4). The term "bore" is often translated "forgiven," as in the case of the "blessed" man of Psalm 32:1.

Besides bearing our "griefs," the Servant carried our "sorrows," the sorrows of despair and death. The Servant, "a man of sorrows and acquainted with grief" (v. 3), Himself took up our griefs and carried our sorrows. He suffered under our load of sin.

The second half of verse 4 mentions the Jews' misunderstanding of His suffering. They considered him "smitten of God, and afflicted" because of His own sin. They thought he was a Sabbath-breaker and a blasphemer (John 5:18). Therefore, they thought His death was a just punishment from God.

The Divine Initiative in His Suffering

Verse 5 explains what happened from God's viewpoint. Far from being a punishment for His own sin, He was wounded for *our* sin. God predetermined Calvary because of our transgressions, and for these the Servant was pierced and crushed.

The contrast between His pain and our blessing is nowhere more vivid than here. He bore the holy wrath of God for the entire sum of all the sins of all the people in the history of the world. Because of His sacrifice, believers are freed from the eternal consequences of their sins, are healed from the guilt of sin, and have perfect peace with the holy God. Note the four statements in verse 5 to explain the Servant's suffering.

The cause of His wounding was our transgressions.
The cause of His bruising was our iniquity.

The result of His punishment was our peace (with God).
The result of His scourging was our healing.

All four of these put together only begin to describe the depths
of His suffering. His wounds were deeper than Roman spikes. His
crushing was heavier than the weight of the cross. His punishment
was more severe than death by crucifixion, His welts more pro-
nounced on His soul than on His back. The real anguish of His
suffering is expressed in the next verse: "The Lord has caused the
iniquity of us all to fall on Him."

> O make me understand it,
> Help me to take it in,
> What it meant to Thee, the Holy One
> To bear away my sin.

The Human Necessity of His Suffering

A future believing Jewish remnant, looking back on the Suffering
Servant, here makes a remarkable confession of their sinful state.
They admit that as sheep follow their leader, so they have followed
the first man into sin; i.e., man is a sinner by nature. They also admit
that each one has "turned to his own way"; i.e., man is a sinner by
personal choice. Both aspects of man's guilt were laid on Christ; the
Good Shepherd bears the sins of wayward "sheep."

Peter's comment on this passage emphasizes the example of the
Suffering Servant (1 Pet. 2:21-25). As He suffered for the undeserv-
ing, so we are to patiently suffer when we are wronged. When
tempted to complain about our trials in service, we are to think back
to Calvary: "Christ also suffered for you, leaving you an example for
you to follow in His steps."

Fourth Stanza: The Servant in Death

His Submission as a Sacrificial Lamb   (53:7)
His Sentence as an Unrighteous Verdict   (53:8)
His Burial as an Honorable Testimony   (53:9)

The Suffering Servant is here seen making the ultimate sacrifice. He was "obedient to the point of death, even death on a cross" (Phil. 2:8). He was treated violently (v. 7). They pushed him from one mockery of a trial to another, pounded him with their fists, and scourged Him with whips. Yet through all this oppression and affliction He never opened His mouth in self-defense, never made a sound. Though pressed by Caiaphas, Pilate, and Herod, the Servant answered nothing (Mark 14:60, 61; 15:3-5; Luke 23:9). He claimed no rights; He called no lawyer. His silence was a measure of His submission to serve, even unto death.

Verse 8 shows that the death sentence passed on Him was an unrighteous verdict: "By oppression and judgment he was taken away." Without the due process of law, He was rushed from Gethsemane through three "trials" and executed. Scarcely ten hours elapsed during the course of His "oppression and judgment" (literally, "detention and judicial proceedings").

"As for his generation who considered . . . " is bettered rendered, "Who of his contemporaries considered?" They didn't realize what was really happening. They missed the purpose of His death, that He was "cut off" as a divine judgment for sin. His work was completely misunderstood, as is often the case with servants of God. We can take comfort from the bitter experience He endured for us.

The ninth verse mentions the Servant's burial. Men assigned His grave to be with criminals and prostitutes. "Yet He was associated with a rich man [singular] in His death" (v. 9). God overruled the plans of men, and Joseph buried Christ's body in his own tomb. God did this for His Servant because "He had done no violence." His sinless life made it fitting that He should be buried with honor, a reward for His humble submission to God's will. This verse testifies to Christ's sinlessness seven centuries before He came.

Fifth Stanza: The Servant Satisfied

Satisfaction from a Finished Work   (53:10b)

Satisfaction from a Justified Believer   (53:11)

Satisfaction from a Deserved Inheritance   (53:12a)[1]

This last stanza is a fitting climax to the "Song of the Suffering Servant," touching on the satisfaction He enjoys as a result of obedient suffering. It is a view of the cross from the throne of God.

The theme begins with a statement of Jehovah's pleasure in bruising (or crushing) the Servant. It is not that Jehovah took pleasure in the Servant's agony, but in the result of His suffering: atonement for sin. The trespass offering, one of five main sacrifices under Levitical law (Lev. 5:14-19), spoke of the demands of God's justice and the required restitution for the harm done. Jesus was our trespass offering as He paid every debt we owed to a holy God by our sin. No doubt His soul sufferings as an offering for sin exceeded His bodily sufferings at the hands of wicked men.

It was His soul being made an offering for sin that brought Him satisfaction. Three aspects of His satisfaction are highlighted here. First, the satisfaction of *completed work*: He sees His "offspring" or posterity. The greatest blessing for a Hebrew man was to see his children and grandchildren, and the Servant sees spiritual sons brought into the family of Jehovah.

Secondly, *His days are prolonged* beyond His suffering and death. This was fulfilled in His resurrection—He is alive forevermore (Rev. 1:18). Then to His prolonged life was added the successful accomplishment of His plan: "The good pleasure [i.e., plan] of the Lord will prosper." Jehovah's salvation-plan had begun in eternity past; now, through the Servant, it was brought to completion.

Third, the Servant's satisfaction came from the delight He felt in *bringing to birth many sons* (v. 11). The imagery here is of travail and birth. As a mother finds delight at the sight of her newborn child, so in His "knowledge" He saw that many sons would come to glory and He was satisfied. As the righteous Servant, He procured righteousness for many. As the risen Savior, he declares them righteous (justified) because He bore their iniquities. To see these former sinners now standing perfect in the sight of a holy God brings Him perfect satisfaction.

This is a well-deserved inheritance. The "portion" He receives from Jehovah is the fruit of His victory on the cross. Because the Servant justified many (v. 11), Jehovah now rewards Him by presenting them to Him as His inheritance. (The word "many" in verse 11 is the same word as "great" in verse 12.) Jehovah also gives Him the "nations" for an inheritance (Ps. 2:8).

The Servant divides the spoil with the strong (the redeemed). That is, having been awarded the believers as His inheritance, He makes them partners in His Kingdom. They are "fellow-heirs" with Him (Rom. 8:16, 17).

---

[1]Verses 10a and 12b are two final views of the Suffering Servant which are background for the Servant's satisfaction.

EIGHT

"A Ransom for Many"

Each of the Gospel writers emphasized one of the four previews of Messiah seen throughout the Old Testament. Matthew focused on His kingship, Luke His manhood, John His Deity. But Mark enlarged on the servant character of Messiah.

Mark's biography of Christ is a unique record of the most perfect servant who ever graced Planet Earth. And His servanthood is the standard for ours. "Have this attitude in yourselves which was also in Christ Jesus, who . . . emptied Himself, taking the form of a bond-servant" (Phil. 2:5, 6).

Mark, the Servant Writer

Mark was uniquely qualified to write about the perfect Servant. We first see him at a prayer meeting when Peter was miraculously released from prison. His mother, a widow, evidently used their spacious home as a meeting-place for the early Jerusalem believers (Acts 12:12-17). Later Barnabas and Saul visited Jerusalem on the "famine visit" and then returned to Antioch in Syria with Mark accompanying them. Mark was apparently an apprentice in the work of evangelism (Acts 12:25). A year later Mark was taken with them on their first missionary journey, specifically as their helper (Acts 13:5). Mark was learning to be a servant. Later he left Paul and Barnabas for an unstated reason, returning to Antioch.

When Paul and Barnabas disagreed over taking Mark a second time and parted ways, Mark went with Barnabas, and nothing is recorded of him for many years until Paul sends his greetings from Rome (Col. 4:10; Philem. 24). By that time there had been reconciliation, for Mark is now mentioned as a "fellow-worker" of Paul's. Finally, Paul appeals to Timothy shortly before his death to bring Mark, "for he is useful to me for service" (2 Tim. 4:11). Mark had learned to serve with the great apostle, and God later used him to write the Gospel of the Servant.

The Servant Theme

Mark was probably the spiritual son of Peter (1 Pet. 5:13) and was almost certainly addressing his Gospel to Romans while living himself in Rome shortly after the death of that apostle. He frequently uses Latin terms such as "centurion" and "legion" and appeals to the Latin mind in recording the activities and work of Christ (whereas the Greeks were more interested in the ideas of Christ, and Jews in the Messianic prophecies). Mark presents Christ to the Roman Gentiles as the active Servant accomplishing His goals, as the disciplined Servant refusing to be turned aside, and as the obedient Servant always doing the will of His Father.

The theme of the Gospel supports Mark's purpose: to convince Romans that Jesus Christ is Deity, the Son of God (1:1). The central statement of the Gospel gives us a simple outline: "For even the Son of Man did not come to be served, but to serve, and to give His life a ransom for many" (10:45).

A comparative study of Mark with the other Gospels will demonstrate Mark's emphasis on Christ's servanthood in many ways. The word "minister" or "ministered" (or "serve" or "served") is used more in Mark than in either Matthew or Luke. Conversely the word "Lord" is used only sixteen times in Mark, as compared with seventy and ninety times respectively in Matthew and Luke; Mark does not call Jesus "Lord" until the very last two verses. Mark omits facts which are inconsistent with the servant theme. There is no visit of the Magi on their kingly quest, no record of genealogy—it is the Servant's work, not his pedigree, which matters. No confounding of the theological doctors in the Temple as a boy of twelve.

Twelve of the sixteen chapters begin with the word "and," showing continuous action. The word "immediately" is used ten times in the first chapter and another thirty times after that. Mark continually portrays the active Servant who always has work to do. As we study our wonderful Servant through Mark's eyes, we full-heartedly admire and adore Him.

The Divine Servant

Wanting to prove to his Roman readers that the Servant he is describing is none other than the Son of God, Mark begins with, "The beginning of the gospel of Jesus Christ, the Son of God" (1:1). We are to see the service Christ rendered in the light of who He was. More than a remarkable person doing wonderful things, He was the mighty Servant of Jehovah, the Son of God.

At Christ's baptism the Father acknowledged this fact: "Thou art My beloved Son" (1:11). Christ Himself claimed that as Son He had authority to forgive sins (2:10). The demons acknowledged His authority as well (3:11). At the cross the centurion exclaimed, "Truly this man was the Son of God" (15:39). Remember, the centurion was a Roman, and it was Mark's purpose for Romans (Gentiles) to come to know who Christ really was.

What a striking contrast—that the majesty of Christ's Sonship should be placed alongside the humility of His servanthood. How this highlights the marvels of His character! But there is a practical side of this truth for all of us who would be servants like Him. We too are called "sons of God" (Rom. 8:14) and have a dignity far beyond anything else in the world. The Apostle John marvels, "See how great a love the Father has bestowed upon us, that we should be called children of God; and such we are" (1 John 3:1). Paul adds, "And if children, heirs also, heirs of God and fellow-heirs with Christ" (Rom. 8:17). Yet, with all that dignity, we are also servants and are to take a lowly place as the perfect Servant did.

The Working Servant

Mark's emphasis on Jesus as Servant is seen also in his portrayal of Him as a worker. Mark alone refers to Jesus as "the carpenter" (Mark 6:3), and it was in this capacity that Christ spent a great part of His earthly life. For perhaps fifteen years the saw, plane, and hammer were His tools. His example will always protect the dignity of honest work, the example of the perfect Servant standing at the carpenter's bench skillfully making yokes for farmers and tables for homes.

Every artisan is a servant, in most cases working for another and in every case working for the ultimate consumer. The good worker, then, has an attitude which is concerned with others and their needs. In working for the foreman he will seek to do everything that is expected of him, even if other workers are not. He will find delight in making consumers happy with a well-made product.

Many Greeks and Romans thought that manual labor was fit only for slaves. Jesus put the lie to that false notion. As James Stalker said: "The virtue of work is that it stamps brute earth with the signature of mind which is the image of Him who is the Supreme Reason." In his book he goes on to use the example of Antonio Stradivari, the famous violin-maker. Stradivari felt called by God to make the best violins, while others criticized him for not "saving the masses." Stalker quotes from T. S. Eliot's poem:

> Who draws a line and satisfies his soul,
> Making it crooked where it should be straight?
> But, God be praised,
> Antonio Stradivari has an eye
> That winces at false work and loves the true,
> With hand and arm that play upon the tool
> As willingly as any singing bird
> Sets him to sing his morning roundelay,
> Because he likes to sing and likes the song.
>
> Then Naldo: " 'Tis a petty kind of fame
> At best, that comes of making violins;
> And saves no masses either. Thou wilt go
> to purgatory none the less."
>
> (Stradivari replies)
> " 'Twere purgatory here to make them ill;
> And for my fame—when any master holds
> 'Twixt chin and hand a violin of mine,

> He will be glad that Stradivari lived,
> Made violins and made them of the best.
> The masters only know whose work is good:
> They will choose mine; and while God gives them skill,
> I give them instruments to play upon,
> God choosing me to help Him."

When Jesus left the carpenter's bench and became a prophet and a teacher, He gave the same dignity to the professional realm that He had given to the artisan's bench. To Him the difference between blue collar and white collar is one of calling, not of quality. In both He was the Servant doing His work with excellence; in both He is the example for us. He practiced in service everything He preached to His disciples.

The Model Servant

"For even the Son of Man did not come to be served, but to serve, and to give His life a ransom for many" (10:45). The setting of this statement is worth noting. Jesus was on His way toward Jerusalem. He had just told the disciples for the third time that He would be condemned to death by the Jews, delivered over to the Gentiles, mocked, spit upon, scourged, and killed; three days later He would rise from the dead (10:33, 34). James and John obviously weren't listening—they asked for the two most important positions in the Kingdom, which they thought would be immediately established. Jesus rebuked them gently, telling them they were asking for much more than they realized.

The other ten disciples, probably of the same mind as James and John, were indignant toward the brothers. They wondered how they could dare ask such a thing. Jesus knew their thoughts and called them all to Himself to explain one of the most important principles of Christian discipleship (10:42-45). Jesus reminded them that among the Gentiles the greatest people had the most authority over others, but that it would be entirely different among His disciples; the greatest among them would be the slave of the others!

Jesus cited His own life as the ultimate example of true discipleship. His great purpose in coming to earth, His whole goal in life, was not to be served by others, but to serve them. He was free from self-interest of any kind. This was not a popular idea in 30 A.D., nor is it today. Dale Carnegie did not include this concept in *How to Win Friends and Influence People*. But the Lord Jesus Christ called it the very essence of discipleship. Serving others is the foundation of the golden rule: "Do unto others as you would have them do unto you."

"I Am Among You as the One Who Serves" (Jesus)

Practically all of Christ's work had to do with service to others. His meek and gentle character was out-of-tune with the arrogance of a society built on power. He told His followers, "Take My yoke upon you, and learn from Me, for I am gentle and humble in heart" (Matt. 11:29). The trouble is, hardly anyone wants to learn. We are too busy pushing ourselves up the ladder of worldly values. This isn't exclusively the game of ambitious disciples either. Self-seeking is seen in the nursery as infants squabble over a toy. Children fight over playing first base in a ballgame. High school girls scratch and scream trying to get exclusive rights to a certain boy. College men cheat in exams so they will appear smarter than the competition. Nations, outraged if they feel their national pride has been hurt, go to war. Humble service? Who thinks about that?

It would be difficult to total up the failure, unhappiness, discontent, and depression that comes from wanting to be served and not being willing to serve. In our culture we are brought up to expect others to minister to us. Our parents should pamper us, our teachers should pass us, our peers should recognize us. We wrongly see these things as our right. So Sunday school teachers quit when they are not profusely thanked, missionaries come home when it appears that nothing is happening, and people change churches when they don't get the recognition they think they deserve.

If only we took the words of Jesus seriously and lived them! My grandfather, a godly man and a spiritual giant, used to sing in his raspy voice, "O to be nothing." As a boy I thought this very strange. Now I understand that he wanted to be more like His Savior whom he loved. He was seeking to respond to the word of Jesus, "Whoever wishes to be great among you shall be your servant" (10:43). Jim Elliot, missionary in the eastern jungle of Ecuador, martyred trying to bring the gospel to the Aucas, had a provocative definition of a missionary: "Missionaries are a bunch of nobodies trying to exalt Somebody." He had grasped the essence of Biblical servanthood.

Mark's Portrait of the Servant

The Gospel of Mark can be looked at as Mark's portrait of Jesus the perfect Servant. As with any good painting the more carefully it is studied, the more its detail and design are appreciated. A large print of Rembrandt's *Jeremiah* hangs in my office at home. Every once in a while I discover another detail which was designed by the artist but only recently discovered by me. I will probably continue to find others for a long time. Mark's word-picture of Jesus is like that. Let us look at some of the beautiful details which he included.

Christ was a Servant with a *mission*. He had a clear understanding of what He was doing and efficiently worked toward fulfillment. To the public He preached the gospel (1:4). He called potential disciples to commitment (1:17, 18). To the Jews in the synagogue He taught with authority (1:22). To the demon-possessed He brought immediate deliverance (1:25). To the sick He gave healing (1:31, 34). All of these fit together as part of the Servant's work in completing His mission.

He was a *diligent* Servant. "In the early morning, while it was still dark, He arose and went out and departed to a lonely place, and was praying there" (1:35). He found it expedient to lose sleep to get the job done. That may challenge many of us who love sleeping in.

But his diligence was balanced by His understanding the need for rest. When He and the disciples had been going hard at it for a long time, at the appropriate moment He recommended that they get away for a time of recharging their physical, mental and spiritual batteries: "Come away by yourselves . . . and rest a while" (6:31).

Our Lord's servanthood was also marked by *compassion*. Looking on a leper, He was "moved with compassion" (1:41). Seeing the multitude as sheep without a shepherd, "He felt compassion for them" (6:34). Love has always been one of the greatest motivators for service, and He loved as no one else ever has. When the multitude had been with Him three days without food, His compassion was demonstrated again as He fed them (8:1-9).

This love, however, never ignored sin in the lives of His hearers.

He called the Pharisees and scribes "hypocrites." Shining the light of the Scriptures, He showed that their hearts were far from God and their worship was vain (7:6, 7).

Mark takes care to point out the *excellence* of everything done by the Lord. After He healed the deaf-mute, the people were utterly astonished and gladly acknowledged that "He has done all things well" (7:37). So many of us who would be His servants and serve others have "feet of clay" in some area. We acknowledge our weaknesses and even allow for them. We should, however, also be constantly striving for the excellence which was seen in the Lord Jesus.

Faith was another characteristic of our Savior. One example will have to suffice. During the storm, when the disciples were frantic with terror, thinking they were all to drown, "He Himself was in the stern asleep" (4:38). The great Servant was resting in faith that a powerful God was in control. When the storm was stilled with a word from Christ, He turned to the relieved disciples and asked them, "How is it that you have no faith?" They had just seen an unforgettable example of trust in the Father. We ought to be praying, as the disciples did on another occasion, "Lord, increase our faith" (Luke 17:5).

Another detail in the portrait is Christ's *willingness* to serve all peoples. Even a Gentile woman of Syrophoenician descent asked for and received healing for her demon-possessed daughter (7:26). Unlike the Pharisees, He loved and served all with whom He came into contact, and true servants will be like Him. He commissioned His own to go into *all* the world and preach the gospel to *every* creature (16:15).

The Suffering Servant

Mark, more than the other Evangelists, describes the events of redemption. The reason for this is that redemption in Mark's Gospel is the work of the Servant. "The Son of Man [came] . . . to give His life a ransom for many" (10:45). The greatest work of the greatest Servant was to redeem man from the slavery of sin.

The Gospel of Mark directly links Christ's suffering on the cross with Isaiah 53, a prophecy about the Suffering Servant. "They crucified two robbers with Him; one on the right and one on the left.

And the Scripture was fulfilled which says, 'He was reckoned with transgressors' " (15:27, 28; Isa. 53:12). Mark alone makes this connection. Then the Messiah's great cry of abandonment, "My God, My God, why hast Thou forsaken Me?" (15:34), links His suffering with Psalm 22:1. That is another of the central Old Testament passages on the sufferings of Christ. The path of the Servant was a path of suffering. Thus His work was accomplished and our redemption secured.

We cannot enter into His redeeming work, no matter how we suffer. But we can be encouraged by His attitude and behavior in His sufferings. Peter develops this theme for literal slaves and for servants of Christ:

> Servants, be submissive to your masters with all respect, not only to those who are good and gentle, but also to those who are unreasonable. For this finds favor, if . . . a man bears up under sorrows when suffering unjustly. . . . For you have been called for this purpose, since Christ also suffered for you, leaving you an example for you to follow His steps, who committed no sin, nor was any deceit found in His mouth; and while being reviled, He did not revile in return; while suffering, He uttered no threats, but kept entrusting Himself to Him who judges righteously. (1 Pet. 2:18-23)

For centuries mistreated servants of God have found courage through the example of the Suffering Servant, boldness to battle through an impossible situation when they were being persecuted for His sake. What, after all, are the sufferings of the moment in the light of Calvary? Peter goes on to challenge us, "since Christ has suffered in the flesh, arm yourselves also with the same purpose . . . so as to live . . . for the will of God" (1 Pet. 4:1).

Mark then has given us the best of all servant models. We can only be enriched as we examine the One who came not to be served but to serve and to give His life a ransom for us.

"I am among you as the one who serves." (Jesus, Luke 22:27)

NINE

Our Humble Savior

The servant character of the Lord Jesus Christ was demonstrated by an act of humility which shocked His disciples, then was used as an example for their ministry to each other: "For I gave you an example that you also should do as I did to you" (John 13:15).

The scene in John 13 is the upper room in which the Passover meal (The Last Supper) had been prepared, on the night Christ was betrayed. This was the last occasion on which the twelve disciples were together with the Lord Jesus. For three and a half years they had learned His ways and followed His steps. On at least three occasions He had told them plainly that He would give His life as a ransom, that He would suffer and be killed and depart out of the world. They loved Him, but were obsessed with the prominent part they expected to play in positions of leadership in a literal kingdom they thought He came to establish at that time.

Who Is the Greatest?

They were so confused about the timing of the Messianic Kingdom and their own role in it that even as they entered the upper room they were arguing about who among them was the greatest (Luke 22:24). Like hens in a farmyard, they pecked at each other to get the best morsels. Isn't that just like us? Our outlook is so self-oriented that we are constantly looking for first pick. Such an attitude is not servant mentality, which looks to the needs of others.

The Lord rebuked their dispute about who was to be the greatest with these words:

> "The kings of the Gentiles lord it over them; and those who have authority over them are called 'Benefactors.' But not so with you, but let him who is the greatest among you become as the youngest, and the leader as the servant. . . . I am among you as the one who serves." (Luke 22:25-27)

One by one they took their places around the table, reclining on the couches. Evidently there was no house slave on hand to do the customary foot washing. An earthenware jar of water was nearby with basin and towel, but none of the disciples made a move to serve the others in this way. They were above this job for the lowliest. But Jesus wasn't.

A Savior Who Serves

The Apostle John tells us that when Jesus washed His disciples' feet He knew four things which make His act all the more remarkable.

First, we are told that He knew that "His hour had come" (v. 1), the time for His suffering and departure from the world. This "hour" was a fixed point in time planned from before the foundation of the world. The world had rejected Him and was soon to crucify Him. When that happened, He would go to the Father. Several times John recorded that "His hour had not yet come" (John 2:4; 7:30; 8:20). But now, on the eve of the crucifixion, His hour had arrived, the hour He would depart out of "this world."

Note that He wasn't leaving "*the* world," but "this world." Evidently the world to Him was a terrible place, full of the effects of sin. Now, in the light of His soon departure from this world by way of death, He humbled Himself and washed their feet. At that key point, with the end near, He did what we would never have done: He accepted a position of humility and slavery. What grace He displayed for His own!

Second, "having loved His own who were in the world, *He*

loved them to the end" (v. 1). His disciples were called "His own" because He delighted to claim them as belonging to Him. He knew them as mere men who had already failed a number of times and would again. He knew that Philip would misunderstand Him around that table. He knew that Peter would deny Him that same night. He knew that Thomas would doubt His resurrection, and that they all would forsake Him and run away before dawn. Yet, knowing all that, He loved them to the very end (literally "to the utmost"). Knowing their flaws, He stooped down in love and washed their dusty feet. He took the form of a servant.

Third, "And during supper, the devil having already put into the heart of Judas Iscariot, the son of Simon, to betray Him . . ." (v. 2). *Jesus was fully aware that the betrayer was sitting at that table* (cf. v. 21). He saw that in the dark recesses of Judas' mind the betrayal plot was being worked out. Aware of all this, the Model Servant bowed to take the feet of Judas in His hands to wash them—a remarkable example of perfect servanthood.

Last, verses 3 and 4 state, "Jesus, knowing that the Father had given all things into His hands, and that He had come forth from God, and was going back to God, rose from super." *Jesus was fully conscious of His divine origin and coming glory.* He knew the Father had promised Him authority over all things in the universe. Yet, the Heir of all things humbled Himself to do the work of a slave. "Have this attitude in yourselves which was also in Christ Jesus" (Phil. 2:5).

The beauty of Christ's self-humbling act is next described by John in a series of meaningful phrases:

> [He] rose from supper,
> and laid aside His garments:
> and taking a towel, he girded Himself about.
> Then He poured water into the basin,
> and began to wash the disciples' feet,
> And to wipe them with the towel. (vv. 4, 5)

These actions are a "parable" of the perfect Servant's work of redemption as described in Philippians 2:5-8. He rose from His place at the Father's side in Heaven. He laid aside the outward aspect of

His glory. He assumed the form of a servant. He poured out His blood as an offering for sin. Then He rose and was seated at the right hand of the Father (see v. 12).

The disciples, however, did not recognize this "parable." Each in his heart no doubt felt that the Lord was the last one among them who should be doing the work of a household slave. Yet, none of them made a move to do the job in His place. Perhaps each thought another of the Twelve should do it. James might have wondered why Andrew didn't accept the task, etc. While they were wondering, Jesus simply continued to wash their feet one by one—until He came to Peter.

Jesus at Peter's Feet

Embarrassed by the whole situation, appalled at what the Lord was doing, Peter didn't comprehend that the Lord never acted outside the worth of His position. On another occasion Peter had rebuked the Lord for speaking of the cross. That time the Lord reminded Peter that he was aligning himself with Satan, because he was not setting his mind on God's interest but man's (Mark 8:33).

Peter now blurted out, "Lord, do You wash my feet?" (v. 6). Why should the Master serve the servant? The Lord's answer (v. 7) indicated that there was more to this than literal water and clean feet: "What I do you do not realize now; but you shall understand hereafter." Peter should be observing and learning, not talking. Later Peter was to learn two valuable spiritual lessons related to this event. One was a lesson on cleansing when he was restored after his threefold denial of the Lord. The other was a lesson on the humility of serving, about which he wrote many years later (1 Pet. 5:1-6).

Peter did not respond to Jesus' words by putting out his feet to be washed. Instead, he tucked them in closer and declared, "Never shall You wash my feet" (v. 8). Peter was evidently humble enough to feel that Jesus should not wash his feet, yet proud enough to instruct the Lord on what not to do. He emphatically stated that Jesus would *never* wash his feet, but sixty seconds later had to change his mind. Like Peter, we are often quick on the trigger when we think we are right, but soon have to look for the "bullet" mistakenly fired.

The Lord gently pointed out to Peter one of the great lessons of foot washing: the benefits of spiritual cleansing. "If I do not wash you, you have no part with Me," Jesus told Peter (v. 8). The Lord was using Peter's soiled feet as an illustration of an important spiritual truth. Just as those feet needed to be cleansed by the household slave because they were dirty, so believers, spiritually defiled by the world, need cleansing. As it was necessary for Peter to admit that his feet were soiled and to place them in the hands of the Lord for cleansing, so the believer who has sinned comes to the Lord, confesses his sin, and receives forgiveness and cleansing.

Jesus told Peter that if he was not washed he would have no "part" with Him. "Part" has reference to daily communion and fellowship with Christ, not to eternal life. The same word is used when Jesus told Martha that Mary had chosen the "good part" (Luke 10:42), because Mary chose to stay in the presence of Christ, while Martha was busy with other things. Our practical communion with Christ is so fragile that the smallest sin can break it. That is why this lesson is so important for all of us who would serve Him.

Luther said, "The Devil allows no Christian to reach Heaven with clean feet all the way." He was right. But the broken fellowship caused by soiled feet can be restored by the cleansing Christ offers. "If we confess our sins, He is faithful and righteous to forgive us our sins and cleanse us from all unrighteousness" (1 John 1:9).

When Peter finally began to see that the Lord was speaking about spiritual cleansing and fellowship with Him, he answered with characteristic impulsiveness. "Lord," he said, "if it is fellowship You are talking about, give me a full bath" (see v. 9). So the Lord explains why Peter only needed his feet washed, and not his whole body (v. 10).

The Lord Jesus used the imagery of the public baths, common in the towns of that day. After bathing, the people returned home along the dusty streets wearing sandals. On reaching home, they found it necessary to have their feet washed. Likewise when they went to the market or visited a friend. There was one bath but many washings of soiled feet. Different Greek words for "bathed" and "wash" in verse 10 corroborate this distinction.

The lesson to Peter, and to us, is that he was already bathed (a believer in Christ, forgiven of all his sins) and did not need that bath repeated. What he did need was cleansing from the defilement of the world (his feet washed). When he sinned, he didn't need salvation but renewal of fellowship with God. It was important for Peter to learn this right at that time, for within a few hours he would commit the worst sin of his life in denying the Lord. Even then, he did not need another bath of salvation, but cleansing and the restoration of fellowship. Part of that story is not recorded, and part is written in John 21. All of it, however, is based on the fact that Christ loved Peter to the uttermost (v. 1).

This provision of spiritual foot washing for the Christian is wonderful. When we sin we can go to the Savior for restoration. He uses the water of the Word to do this (Eph. 5:26). When we are aware of having displeased Him, we can go immediately to Him in confession. Then the perfect Servant graciously performs His work of washing our feet, and fellowship with Him is again a present reality. We cannot be effective servants of Christ if we have unwashed feet.

Of course, one of the Twelve had never had the bath of regeneration. That was Judas, and Jesus is careful to point this out (vv. 10, 11). Then from verses 12 to 17 the Lord teaches them another important lesson from His acted-out parable, a lesson directly associated with learning how to serve. When He had finished His act of service, He took His place at the table and began to teach a lesson to all of them. His lesson to Peter had been on the believer's vertical relationship with Him. Now He talks about a horizontal relationship, that of the disciples to one another.

He began with the question, "Do you know what I have done to you?" (v. 12). Without waiting for an answer He explained, "You call Me Teacher and Lord; and you are right, for so I am. If I then, the Lord and the Teacher, washed your feet, you also ought to wash one another's feet. For I gave you an example that you also should do as I did to you" (vv. 13-15).

The Lord Jesus was saying in effect, "If I, your Lord and Master, have taken the role of a servant, then you who are My servants should be willing to be servant to each other." This is logical but so difficult. They would gladly have washed His feet, but He insists that they serve their fellowman.

The point here is not just humble service, but specifically cleansing the soiled feet of others. Paul referred to this ministry in Galatians 6:1—"Brethren, even if a man is caught in any trespass, you who are spiritual, restore such a one in a spirit of gentleness; looking to yourself, lest you too be tempted." If a brother is caught in a sin such as pride or gossip or . . . , spiritual people acting as true servants are to restore him, esteeming him more important than themselves (Phil. 2:3). They are to "wash his feet." How? By taking the "water" of the Word of God and gently, ever so gently, applying it to their brother and his sin, all the time being aware that they too are vulnerable to temptation.

The tendency of the flesh is to do this harshly or with a superior attitude; to use boiling water so he won't forget, to use sandpaper instead of the pure water of the Word. The Christian community is filled with people with soiled feet. Only genuine servants, humble, spiritual, and wise through the work of the Holy Spirit, can restore them.

The Lord's act was self-denying service. He practiced what He preached when He told the disciples that He came to serve rather than be served (Mark 10:45). They would remember what He did that evening for as long as they lived. Twenty-five years later when Peter wrote his first epistle, he echoed the Master's message on foot washing, urging church elders to prove themselves examples to the flock, not lording it over them but humbling themselves under the mighty hand of God (1 Pet. 5:3, 6). Peter learned that lesson well. Have we?

A Beatitude

The Savior's lesson on service closed with a beatitude: "If you know these things, you are blessed if you do them" (v. 17). Like the beatitudes in Matthew 5, this blessing from God comes as a result of obedience to Him. God has a special blessing for the humble servant who lowers himself to "wash the feet" of his fellow-servants. As a "doer of the word" he will be blessed in what he does (James 1:22, 25).

What needless pain is ours because we refuse to humble ourselves and serve as "foot washers." If we regard such service to be beneath our dignity, we are placing ourselves above Him. Jesus told His disciples that "a slave is not greater than his master" (v. 16), and His true servants should not shrink from doing what He did. Diotrephes would not have failed if he had heeded Jesus' words (3 John 9). Sad chapters in church history might have been avoided as well, and many divisions would not be happening in churches today.

With hurting Christians all around us, there is plenty of room for the service of foot washing. We have every encouragement from the Lord Jesus Himself to do it; in fact, we have His command. If we would truly follow the Master, we will walk in lowly paths of service.

> O Master, let me walk with Thee
>   In lowly paths of service free,
> Tell me Thy secret; help me bear
>   The strain of toil, the fret of care.
>
> Help me the slow of heart to move
>   By some clear, winning word of love,
> Teach me the wayward feet to stay,
>   And guide them in the homeward way.
>   (Washington Gladden)

PART THREE

PORTRAITS

TEN

God's Inner Circle

God's greatest people have always been servants. The title "servant of God," the most distinguished in the story of the Bible, the title of those who were the key people in God's master plan for Planet Earth, still belongs to all who truly walk with God. In Old Testament times God bestowed it only on those spiritual giants who pioneered the life of faith. We will focus on them in this chapter.

The term "servant of God" in the Old Testament has more to do with the relationship of the individual to God than to other people. There was no concept then of a leader or king being a "public servant" as we use the term today (1 Kings 12:7 is an exception). God seems to take pleasure in giving the title "My servant" to those who honor Him with full allegiance.

The Believing Servant:
"My Servant Abraham"

The first of the Bible greats whom God called "My servant" was Abraham, and God used the title while talking to Abraham's son, Isaac.

In his bedouin-type life Isaac had constant trouble with getting water for his large flocks. He dug wells, but there were quarrels over their use. Or the Philistines would stop them up to keep Isaac's men away from their borders. Eventually he arrived in Beersheba and dug yet another well (Gen. 26:18-25). His father Abraham had taken him to live in Beersheba after the great offering on Mount Moriah. Isaac had been released and the ram offered as a substitute sacrifice, and God then confirmed His promise to Abraham (Gen. 22:1-19). Now when Isaac returned to Beersheba to live, God appeared to him and confirmed His promise that Isaac would be blessed and that his descendants would be many. The reason God did this was "for the sake of My servant Abraham" (Gen. 26:24).

God called Abraham His servant because he had dared to believe God and act accordingly. When the God of glory appeared to him while he was an idol-worshiping heathen in Ur, a city of Chaldea, and told him to leave his relatives and go to a place he had never seen—he did it. He was obedient.

Also, when God promised to bless Abraham materially, Abraham believed that God would do it! He cheerfully allowed Lot to choose the well-watered plain of Sodom. He cheerfully rejected taking anything at all from the King of Sodom after a rescue operation. As a servant of God he did not want anyone to say that they had made him rich (Gen. 14:22, 23). It was Abraham who used the name Adonai (Lord) for the first time (Gen. 15:2). This title for God expresses His Lordship; it is the servant's title for the Master.

Even when God tested Abraham's faith and commanded him to offer his son Isaac as a burnt offering, Abraham obeyed without question. "So Abraham rose early in the morning and saddled his donkey" (Gen. 22:3). His whole life was marked by serving God unreservedly. He dared to believe God and act on it. It is no surprise that God conferred on him the honor of being called "My servant Abraham."

The Confident Servant: "Have You Considered My Servant Job?"

Job lived in antiquity, exactly when no one knows. A certain amount of mystery surrounds him, which makes his history all the more fascinating. In the book of Job we are reminded both at the beginning and at the end that Job was called "My servant" by God (1:8; 42:7).

In the introduction to the book God asked His enemy Satan if he had considered Job, His servant, as an example of a godly believer

(1:8). At this point God gave Satan permission to tempt Job in various ways in order to prove that Job's happy servanthood was based on more than material prosperity. Notice how God described Job, His "servant": "For there is no one like him on the earth, a blameless and upright man, fearing God and turning away from evil" (1:8).

True servants are known for what they are as well as what they do. Nothing whatever was said of Job's activity as a servant; the emphasis was on what he was in his character. God said that there was not another man like him in all the earth; he was a model of human righteousness. In relation to evil, Job not only was blameless himself—he actively shunned it. In relation to God, he was upright and actively and reverently sought Him.

The writer of Job noted these same characteristics in the very first verse, and God challenged Satan with them a little later (1:1, 8). They are connected with the quality of Job as a servant of God. Servants must *be* servants before they can *perform* as servants. All the temptations and trials which followed could not shake Job, because he was a true servant of God in his heart, and this was the secret of Job's integrity through all of his temptations. Though he did not understand what was happening, he never lost his confidence in God. He remained a true servant.

When it was all over, Job spoke of "things too wonderful for me" (42:3). Instead of finding that God had forgotten him, he found the power, majesty, and wisdom of God to be more infinite than he had known before, and he fell down in reverent repentance. It was the three "friends" who came in for judgment, and they were instructed to offer a sacrifice to God while "My servant Job" prayed for them (42:8).

We who would be servants must learn from Job that God demands holiness first, last, and always. No amount of activity makes up for lives which are not "blameless and upright, fearing God and turning away from evil."

The Submissive Servant:
"As for Me and My House, We Will Serve the Lord"

God honored Joshua by calling him His servant, but Joshua was unique in that he was also called a servant of a human master,

Moses. Twice in the Bible he is "Joshua . . . the servant of the Lord" and twice he is the servant of Moses (Josh. 24:29; Judg. 2:8; Exod. 33:11; Num. 11:28). Joshua's dual servanthood has something to say to us.

Joshua, evidently recognized for his proficiency in taking and giving orders, was selected by Moses to be his assistant during the exodus from Egypt to Canaan (Exod. 33:11). The first look at Joshua in Scripture is in the posture of obedience to Moses, who asked him to choose an army and fight the Amalekites. "And Joshua did as Moses told him" (Exod. 17:9, 10). That is the "servant" in him. Later he accompanied Moses up Mount Sinai to receive the covenant from God and was also put in charge of the "tent of meeting" where the Lord spoke with Moses from time to time (Exod. 33:11).

Joshua was faithful during the rebellion of the golden calves, in which even Moses' brother Aaron participated. Joshua and Caleb were honored by God for their faithfulness as the only two of the original twelve spies who made it through to the Promised Land.

Joshua the son of Nun
And Caleb the son of Jephunneh
Were the only two who ever got through
To the land of milk and honey.

Having proved his servanthood under Moses, God entrusted Joshua with even greater service when Moses died. As the Lord Jesus taught in the Parable of the Talents, "Well done, good and faithful slave; you were faithful in a few things, I will put you in charge of many things" (Matt. 25:21).

Two incidents in the book of Joshua make a special point of his service. The first of these occurred after the crossing of the Jordan, just prior to the conquest of Canaan (5:13-15). God gave Joshua a vision to confirm His purpose to utterly destroy everything, both man and woman, with "the edge of the sword" (Deut. 20:16, 17; Josh. 6:21). Seeing a man with a sword drawn in his hand, Joshua asked, "Are you for us or for our adversaries?" (v. 13). The swordsman identified Himself as "captain of the host of the Lord," the Commander-in-chief of the universal army of Jehovah.

When Joshua realized who was talking to him in the vision, he "fell on his face to the earth, and bowed down, and said to him, 'What has my lord to say to his servant?' " (v. 14). From here on it would not be the great commander Joshua leading the people to victory, but the *servant* Joshua doing the will of the Divine Commander. Not Joshua's brilliance as a military strategist, but his obedience to God would begin the holy battles for the Promised Land.

The second incident where we especially see Joshua's servanthood is recorded in Joshua 24:14-24. After giving a charge to the leaders who would rule when he was gone (chap. 23), Joshua gave a charge to the people in a great congregational meeting in Shechem (chap. 24). After reminding them of their idolatrous past, he urged them to fear the Lord and serve only Him, to make a definite commitment to serve the Lord: "Choose for yourselves today whom you will serve" (v. 15). To submit to God and serve Him meant rejecting the false gods of those beyond the Euphrates River and of the Canaanites. Joshua then added a personal declaration: "As for me and my house, we will serve the Lord" (v. 15). What a tremendous challenge with which to conclude 110 years of service to God. "Israel served the Lord all the days of Joshua and all the days of the elders who survived Joshua" (24:31).

The example of Joshua inspires us to serve God fully. He learned how to serve at the human level as the servant of Moses, then graduated to greater responsibility under the Divine Commander, emerging as one of the truly great servants of Bible history.

The Loyal Servant:
"My Servant Caleb Has Followed Me Fully"

God's testimony about Caleb is one of the most remarkable in Scriptures: he "fully followed" the Lord. God said this, and Moses, Caleb himself, and Joshua agreed. Five times Scripture confirms that this was the identifying mark of Caleb (Num. 14:24; Deut. 1:36; Josh. 14:8, 9, 14). Who among us would not like God to say that of us?

But notice that the man who followed the Lord fully was called a "servant." This should not surprise us, for what characterizes a servant of the Lord more than "following"? Obedience is the essence of true service. One by one the disciples heard the Lord's invitation, "Follow Me," and they obeyed.

Caleb was from one of the chief families in the tribe of Judah. (His older brother Ram was in the direct line of the Lord Jesus Christ.) Caleb was selected to represent Judah when twelve spies were sent into the land (Num. 13:6). After the majority report by the ten who were so negative about the chances of defeating the Canaanites, Caleb was the spokesman for the minority (himself and Joshua): "We should by all means go up and take possession of it, for we shall surely overcome it. . . . If the Lord is pleased with us, then He will bring us into this land, and give it to us" (Num. 13:30; 14:8). Caleb believed that following the Lord meant taking Him at His word, even when human odds were against them.

Caleb tried to persuade the Israelites, but they would not listen and would in fact have stoned him if the glory of the Lord had not appeared. Moses then prayed a great prayer for forgiveness, and God's answer was that those who had seen His glory in Egypt and had rebelled ten times since would not enter the land of promise. However, about Caleb He said, "But My servant Caleb, because he has had a different spirit and has followed Me fully, I will bring into the land which he entered, and his descendants shall take possession of it" (Num. 14:24). That is exactly what happened.

When they eventually arrived in the Promised Land, Caleb requested as his inheritance the very spot they had spied out forty years before—the area around Hebron, where the giants lived. With God in command and Caleb, now an old man, still "following," his mini-army took those cities, and his family settled there. The servant who followed fully was richly blessed, and the same is true today.

The Faithful Servant:
"My Servant Moses, He is Faithful"
The most frequently mentioned servant in the Old Testament is Moses, probably the greatest among all God's Old Testament leaders. To manage two million people as they journey forty years over trackless wilderness is no mean task. Yet that was Moses' job, requiring as much strength of character as any responsibility ever given a man. Realizing this, it is almost shocking to find him de-

scribed as "very humble ["meek," KJV], more than any man who was on the face of the earth" (Num. 12:3). In this Moses was like the Lord Jesus who said, "I am gentle and humble in heart" (Matt. 11:29).

In the same chapter in which Moses is described as the most humble man who lived on earth, God calls Moses "My servant" (vv. 7, 8). These two facets of Moses' character are seen together in an incident recorded in that same chapter. Miriam, Moses' sister, joined with Aaron in throwing an ethnic slur at Moses because he had married a Cushite. They claimed that they were equally able to fulfill a prophetic ministry. Obviously pride was at work in their hearts, and it is just at this point where God reminds us that Moses was the most humble man on earth (v. 3).

Then God did a remarkable thing, calling Miriam and Aaron out to the tent of meeting outside the camp to give them a lecture. He told them that if they were indeed prophets the Lord would speak through them in visions or dreams, but that Moses was in a higher category: "Not so with My servant Moses, He is faithful in all My household. . . . With him I speak mouth to mouth" (Num. 12:7, 8). God vindicated Moses as being His faithful servant to whom He could speak face to face. Because Miriam had been unfaithful and lacked a servant attitude, God was angry with her and she became a leper. But Moses interceded for her, and God healed her. However, she later died at Kadesh and never reached the Promised Land. Nothing tempts us to lash out more than unfair criticism from our own family. Moses passed such a test with flying colors.

The author of Hebrews calls Jesus "the Apostle and High Priest of our confession" (3:1) and then compares Christ's faithfulness to Moses who was faithful in all his household (v. 2). It is striking that the Lord is compared to a man, but significant that that man is Moses. The passage in Hebrews continues, "Moses was faithful in all his house as a servant" (v. 5). In God's eyes, to be great we must serve.

The Obedient Servant:
"My Servant Isaiah Has Gone Naked"

Isaiah, the prince of the prophets, was one of the select group who were called "My servant" by the Lord. He had a great impact on the little kingdom of Judah during a time of moral decline, warning leaders of the nation who were compromising their faith in God for political power and sensual indulgence. Judgments on the little nation of Judah were certain, but Isaiah directed their attention past those judgments to a coming Kingdom where righteousness and peace will reign.

When Isaiah was called to serve, he saw a vision of a holy God on His throne (Isa. 6). Falling down before that throne, overwhelmed by his own unworthiness, he heard the call from God, "Whom shall I send, and who will go for us?" (v. 8). The prophet answered as any true servant would: "Here am I. Send me!" He was a willing servant, ready to listen, ready to speak, ready to go as the Lord directed. It is fitting that it is to Isaiah that God reveals the marvelous Servant prophecies of the Messiah (42—53).

The circumstances of chapter 20, where God calls him "My servant," are peculiar but instructive. The Assyrian king, Sargon II, was on the warpath in Palestine, where Judah was then one of several small nations. A strong Philistine city, Ashdod, had already fallen to his armies in 721 B.C. The surrounding cities, shaking with fear, were tempted to ally themselves with Egypt in resisting Assyria. Judah's leaders considered the same choice, even though they had been warned by the prophet to trust in God, not Egypt. At this point God told Isaiah to perform an unusual but symbolic action.

The prophet was already dressed in sackcloth, mourning for the nation of Judah under judgment. Now he was told to strip off the sackcloth and his shoes and walk around like that through the streets of Jerusalem for three years (20:2). Isaiah was to demonstrate publicly what Egyptians captured by Assyria would look like. Egypt was going to be defeated by Assyria and captives stripped and marched off to Assyria. Why should Judah trust in Egypt who was going to be defeated?

Isaiah can teach us something about servanthood here. He, as a respected prophet, was asked to do a ridiculous thing—to appear in public dressed only in his underwear. Not just once but regularly for three years, while women whispered, children giggled, and politicians laughed. No matter the laughing critics. God had spoken, and His servant Isaiah would bear the brunt of their jokes. To Isaiah, a "well done" from his Master was better than the applause of the ungodly.

True servants of God are often tested by ridicule. So was the Lord Jesus.

> Bearing shame and scoffing rude,
> In my place condemned He stood,
> Sealed my pardon with His blood,
> Hallelujah, what a Savior.

The Empowered Servant:
"Zerubbabel My Servant"

Zerubbabel, governor of Jerusalem among the returned exiles from Babylon, was also called "My servant" by the Lord (Hag. 2:23). He was born in captivity, in the royal line of David (Matt. 1:12). His main task was to rebuild the Temple which had been destroyed by Nebuchadnezzar seventy years before, and two prophets encouraged him in his work, Haggai and Zechariah. Haggai ended his prophecy with the promise that in a future day Zerubbabel would reign, His signet ring being a symbol of rule and authority (Hag. 2:23). The significance of the prophecy was that Zerubbabel the servant foreshadowed a greater Servant to come, One who would reign on the throne of David.

When Zerubbabel heard the prophet Haggai contrast the comfortable houses of the people with the ruined condition of the Temple (1:7, 8), he "obeyed the voice of the Lord" and began to rebuild the Temple (1:12). God encouraged him not to look at the smallness of the second Temple compared with the first, but rather to remember that what he was doing was part of God's plan and that one day the "glory of this house" would exceed anything in the past (2:4-9). God's promise was a great stimulus to Zerubbabel and should encourage us to avoid discouraging comparisons and trust the Master.

God's servant Zerubbabel was also encouraged by the prophet Zechariah during the rebuilding project: "Not by might nor by power, but by My Spirit" (4:6). Zerubbabel needed to be reminded that human energy and resources were not the principal factors in accomplishing God's work. Is this not still true for us today? Are we not often guilty of relying on arms of flesh instead of the power of God's servants? "But . . . My Spirit, says the Lord of hosts."

The Loving Servant:
"David Served His Own Generation"

Our final Bible character who is called "My servant" by God Himself is David, and that title is used more of him than of any other. God seemed to take special delight in calling David "My servant."

A shepherd boy, David went unnoticed until the prophet Samuel anointed him as the future king. His path from then until his coronation was long and difficult. But during all this time David walked with God humbly as a servant. His failures are well-known, but his faithfulness as a servant also deserves careful attention.

The first time God calls David "My servant" is when He speaks to Nathan the prophet about David's assured place in history and his kingdom that would last forever (2 Sam. 7). This chapter also contains a wonderful prayer by David the servant, including these remarkable words:

> "Who am I, O Lord God, and what is my house, that Thou hast brought me this far?. . .
> Thou hast spoken also of the house of Thy servant concerning the distant future. . . .
> Thou hast done all this greatness to let Thy servant know. . . .
> Thou art great, O Lord God; for there is none like Thee. . . .
> Thou hast established for Thyself Thy people Israel. . . .
> Now therefore, O Lord God, the word that Thou hast spoken concerning Thy servant and his house, confirm it forever. . . .
> May it please Thee to bless the house of Thy servant . . . and with Thy blessing may the house of Thy servant be blessed forever." (vv. 18-29)

It was the condition of David's heart that made him a servant. When King Saul failed, God told Samuel that the Lord was seeking for Himself a man after His own heart (1 Sam. 13:14), and that man was David. God says of him, "I have found David My servant. . . . My arm also will strengthen him. . . . My faithfulness . . . will be with him" (Ps. 89:20-24). A thousand years later Paul quotes from these passages in presenting the gospel to the people of Antioch, and especially mentions David's servant-heart: " 'I have found David the son of Jesse, a man after My heart, who will do all My will.' From the offspring of this man . . . God has brought to Israel a Savior, Jesus" (Acts 13:22, 23). The key to David's greatness was the willingness of his heart to do all the will of God.

Paul made an additional comment about David's service in Acts 13: "For David, after he had served the purpose of God in his own generation, fell asleep" (v. 36). A Biblical servant wants nothing more than to serve the purpose of God in his time. Whether this means obscurity or publicity, foreign service or home service, to be single or married, nothing matters more than to serve our God. May God help us to do it as David did.

The famous poet John Milton, totally blind at the age of forty-four, has given special insight into these matters.

When I consider how my light is spent,
E'er half my days, in this dark world and wide,
And that one talent which is death to hide,
Lodged with me useless, though my Soul more bent
To serve therewith my Maker, and present
My true account, lest He returning chide,
Doth God exact day labor, light denied,
I fondly ask; but Patience, to prevent
That murmur, soon replies, God doth not need
Either man's work or his own gifts. Who best
Bear His mild yoke, they serve Him best. His state
Is Kingly: thousands at his bidding speed,
And post o'er land and ocean without rest;
They also serve who only stand and wait.

("On His Blindness")

ELEVEN

Tales for the Christ-followers

Some of the finest teaching in all of the Bible on the subject of servanthood is that of the Lord Jesus to His disciples in the form of parables. Unless the disciples learned to serve, they would never be effective for the Lord.

In at least eight of His parables the Lord illustrated basic principles of true service. We who would be useful in the work of God should pay close attention.

Responsible Servants Are Accountable

Jesus' Parable of the Faithful Servants (Luke 12:35-48) is about stewards or servants in the household of a wealthy man who had gone to a wedding feast. Because they did not know when the master would return, they were to be on the alert for his coming at any hour and ready to give an account of their actions during his absence. Thus the Lord began the parable by instructing His followers to "Be dressed in readiness, and keep your lamps alight" (v. 35), prepared for the return of the Master at any time. "Be like men who are waiting for their master when he returns . . ." (v. 36).

This parable had a clear lesson for the disciples who were soon to be left in the world when the Lord ascended to Heaven. With the promise of His return they too were to be conducting themselves as servants, ready for service and constantly on the alert with their "lamps alight."

The steward who had been faithful and sensible in doing the will of his master would be rewarded with greater responsibility and privilege (vv. 43, 44). But the steward who acted irresponsibly during the absence of the master would be judged because he knew his master's will but instead misused his privilege and beat other servants in the household, ignoring the coming return of the master. He would be punished with "many lashes" (vv. 45-47).

Jesus is teaching us here that we are responsible to know His will and to be ready for an accounting when He comes. The Lord finishes his parable with the statement: "And from everyone who has been given much shall much be required: and to whom they entrusted much, of him they will ask all the more" (v. 48).

Responsible Servants Consider Eternity

Jesus' Parable of the Unjust Steward, sometimes called the Parable of the Farsighted Manager (Luke 16:1-13), is the story of a servant whose job was to manage the affairs of his master's estate. Accused of squandering his master's possessions and misappropriating them for his own purposes, he was dismissed and instructed to prepare a final accounting. All this leads up to the point of the parable, which is that the servant used the opportunity he had to prepare for the future.

Looking to the future, he secretly made a series of deals with the master's creditors so that they would be his friends after he was discharged. In all probability his master had charged exorbitant and illegal interest, and the unrighteous servant wrote off each creditor's interest and let them pay only the primary debt. The owner was thus put in an awkward position because to repudiate the servant would expose his own dishonesty. The master was outwitted by a smart rogue who was farsighted enough to use present opportunities with an eye to the future.

As Jesus said, "the sons of light" can learn a lesson from "the sons of this age," who use the present to prepare for the future. Jesus made the application, "Make friends for yourselves by means of the Mammon of unrighteousness" (v. 9). Or as the NIV puts it, "Use worldly wealth to gain friends for yourselves." They were to use transient things for eternal benefit.

Mammon (worldly wealth) was never to be the master. "You cannot serve God and Mammon" (v. 13). But Mammon can be used to promote the cause of the Kingdom of God. For example, money can be used to support evangelists or to buy Scriptures for distribution. Thus we will have "friends" in Heaven as a result of wise use of the transient assets of earth.

The Lord ends this parable with the maxim, "No servant can serve two masters. . . . You cannot serve God and Mammon" (v. 13). He had said it before in the context of being anxious about food and clothing (Matt. 6:24, 25). Now He uses it in the context of eternal values. Servants are not to serve Mammon, but to use it for God's glory. As an old chorus says, "May I do each day's work for Jesus, with eternity's values in view."

Responsible Servants Are Diligent

The Parable of the Ten Minas emphasizes a third important principle of true servanthood (Luke 19:11-27), the principle of diligence. As He told this parable, our Lord was approaching Jerusalem with His disciples, who thought that this was to be the time when the literal Kingdom would appear. Knowing this, Jesus told the story of a nobleman who went to another country to be appointed king and would then return. During his absence ten of his servants were given one mina each and were to "Do business with this until I come back" (v. 13). (A mina was worth about a hundred days' wages.) They were to use the minas entrusted to them to further the interests of the nobleman. In time the nobleman returned, having been appointed king in the far country but rejected as king in his own nation. He then called his servants and requested an accounting.

In the parable three of the servants reported on their activities. One of them had gained ten more minas with the one he had received. Another had gained five more. But the third had only kept his in a safe place.

The first two servants were highly commended for their faithfulness by the master and were given places of honor and authority in the kingdom. The third servant, because he had been unwilling to take any risks with the mina, fearing the master's anger if he should lose it, was judged. He had been specifically charged to do business with his mina, and now he could only plead his fear of the master's strictness. His mina was given to the one who had gained ten.

All of us as servants are to be diligent in the Master's business. He Himself demonstrated this as a boy of twelve—"Know ye not that I must be about My Father's business?" (Luke 2:49, KJV). He used available opportunities to bring His Father glory. We too are called upon to "buy up the opportunities" (Eph. 5:16, literal translation). We should remember the instruction of Paul to another servant, Timothy: "Be diligent to present yourself approved to God as a workman who does not need to be ashamed, handling accurately the word of truth" (2 Tim. 2:15).

Responsible Servants Have No Limits

> "But which of you, having a slave plowing or tending sheep, will say to him when he has come in from the field, 'Come immediately and sit down to eat'? But will he not say to him, 'Prepare something for me to eat, and properly clothe yourself and serve me until I have eaten and drunk; and afterward you will eat and drink'? He does not thank the slave because he did the things which were commanded, does he? So you too, when you do all the things which are commanded you, say, 'We are unworthy slaves; we have done only that which we ought to have done.' " (Luke 17:7-10)

This short parable emphasizes the servant's obligation to his master. To what point is he responsible? The parable shows that there are no limits to the servant's duty.

The disciples, realizing that they needed faith to carry out the instructions given them by the Lord, asked Him, "Increase our faith." In His answer the Lord told them that even faith as small as a mustard seed was sufficient to move a mountain (v. 6). He was saying that they didn't need more faith, but needed to exercise the faith they already had. The parable amplifies this thought.

Coming home after a day's work tired and hungry, the servants might expect some time to themselves. Instead the master asks them to prepare his supper and wait on him while he enjoys the evening. The needs and desires of the master take absolute precedence over those of the servants. Jesus asks, "He [the slave owner] does not thank the slave . . . does he?" The answer is no—they had simply done their duty.

Then the Lord applies the parable: "So you too, when you do all the things which are commanded you, say, 'We are unworthy slaves; we have done only that which we ought to have done' " (v. 10). We are to present our body as a "living and holy sacrifice," which is described as our "reasonable service" (KJV) (Rom. 12:1, 2). There are no limits to our responsibility to the Lord Jesus Christ. Giving Him our best, we are merely doing what is our duty.

Responsible Servants Forgive

Jesus' Parable of the Unmerciful Servant points to the principle of forgiveness (Matt. 18:21-35). The parable came in response to a question Peter asked about how often he would forgive someone who had sinned against him. Peter did not wait for the Lord's answer, but quickly suggested that the most spiritual person might forgive an offender "up to seven times." No doubt he thought that was a most generous offer. The Lord quickly popped Peter's balloon by telling him that forgiveness should extend to seventy times seven. Then He told the parable to explain what He meant.

The parable was about a king who wanted to settle his accounts. One of his servants was discovered to owe him ten thousand talents, an astronomical debt which it would be impossible to pay. The king, following the law of the land, sentenced the debtor and his family to be sold into slavery. The poor man prostrated himself before the king, and the king compassionately forgave the whole debt.

The king in the parable represents God. The debtor unable to pay is the sinner. On confession of our spiritual debt, the King has displayed His merciful love in complete forgiveness. Praise God.

The parable goes on to say that the forgiven servant went out to collect a small personal debt from a fellow-servant, an amount which was minuscule compared to the amount he had been forgiven. His fellow-servant begged for time to pay, but was thrown into prison. The forgiven servant showed no mercy at all. When this was reported to the king, he became angry and revoked his forgiveness, throwing the first servant into jail to be punished.

The application is clear though shocking. The servant who understands the great mercy he has been shown at the cross must show forgiveness and mercy to others. Failing to forgive will bring judgment—not the loss of eternal life, but chastisement from a holy God.

As servant of God we will often be on the receiving end of un-Christlike actions and words. These must be forgiven or we cannot have a fruitful ministry for God. Forgiving a person seventy times seven times (i.e., again and again and again) for the same sin seems too much, until it is seen in the light of Calvary. Because we are forgiven sinners, we can forgive others.

True forgiveness is the responsibility of true servants.

Responsible Servants Don't Compare Rewards

The Parable of the Laborers in the Vineyard has much to say to Christ's servants (Matt. 20:1-11). Peter had just asked, "We have left everything and followed You; what then will there be for us?" He obviously assumed that the sacrifices he had made would entitle him to a greater reward than others who had not paid the same price. The Lord gently rebuked Peter by reminding him that coming blessings would far surpass any sacrifices made: "Everyone who has left houses or brothers or sisters . . . shall receive many times as much" (Matt. 19:29). Then He states, both before and after the parable, "But many who are first will be last; and the last, first" (Matt. 19:30; 20:16). The principle of the parable is that God gives rewards according to His sovereign pleasure, not according to man's ideas.

In the story the landowner agreed to pay his workers one denarius a day, the usual wage. Later at the third, the sixth, and the ninth hours, he found others idle and put them to work in his vineyard also. There were even some hired in the eleventh hour, only having to work one hour. In the evening he first paid the last laborers hired. They received one denarius, as did the ninth-, sixth-, and third-hour workers. Those who had worked all day grumbled that they deserved more; they had borne the heat of the day, whereas the others had not.

The answer of the Lord to the grumblers is the point of the whole parable: "Take what is yours and go your way, but I wish to give to this last man the same as you. Is it not lawful for me to do what I wish with what is my own? Or is your eye envious because I am generous?" (vv. 14, 15). It is God's sovereign choice. True fairness must be based on God's justice, for He alone has all the facts.

Servants should refrain from comparing themselves with others and from predetermining what God's reward will be. Many who are first in man's judgment will be last in God's. And the last in man's judgment will be first in God's. Responsible servants don't compare rewards.

Responsible Servants Lead Wisely

As part of the Olivet Discourse the Lord told the Parable of the Wise Servant (Matt. 24:45-51). In this great prophetic message the Lord Jesus was answering the disciples' question about the sign of His coming and the end of the age (v. 3). He explained to them the sign of the "Abomination of Desolation" during the "great tribulation" and that this would be followed by the coming of the Son of Man in power and great glory (vv. 15-31). Next came the Parable of the Fig Tree and a history lesson from the days of Noah. From this they learned that the general time would be clear, but the exact day and hour would not (vv. 32-41). (The completed ark was a general sign. The exact day was unknown.)

The disciples were told to be on the alert, therefore, because they did not know the time of Christ's return. But they were also to be responsibly active in doing the will of the Master. As servants they were never to neglect their duty, especially in relation to those under their authority. In the parable they had the responsibility to feed and to properly guide the household (v. 45).

Leadership was their responsibility while the Master was absent, but they were to not to misuse the authority they had over others. They were to be unselfish and caring, unlike the wicked servant who said, "My master is not coming for a long time," so dared to mistreat the others (vv. 48, 49). A faithful and wise servant considered the needs and weaknesses of those under his authority. He kept in view the return of the master and wanted to win approval from him.

The primary application of this parable was to servants in the time of the "great tribulation" who will be expecting the coming of the Lord in power and great glory. But the principle of servanthood here is equally applicable to us. The Lord Jesus told Peter to "Tend My lambs . . . Tend My sheep" (John 21:15-17). Peter was not to be concerned with what John or anyone else was to do. He had his own responsibility until the Lord returned.

In the parable the alternative to caring leadership was the stern judgment of the Lord upon His return (vv. 50, 51). How important it is, therefore, for us to discharge our responsibility wisely and faithfully. Leadership will be part of our service for Christ whether as a mother with her children or as an employer or a leader in the local church or . . . Understanding and unselfishness are to mark that leadership.

Responsible Servants Use Their Talents

The Parable of the Talents, found in Matthew 25:14-30, was part of the Lord's Olivet Discourse on the subject of the coming of Messiah and the responsibility of those who wait for Him. In the preceding Parable of the Ten Virgins (vv. 1–13), the subject had been expectant preparation. In this parable the emphasis is on serving rather than on watchfulness.

The master is pictured in the parable as going on a journey and entrusting three of his servants with varied responsibilities to match their differing abilities. One was given five talents, one was given two, and a third was given only one. During the absence of the master each was expected to increase his talent or talents.

The difference between this parable and the Parable of the Minas (Luke 19) lies in what the servants started with. Minas referred to basics such as time, opportunity, and life itself; in these we all have the same amount. In the Parable of the Talents the differing *talents* refer to things such as personality, physical strength, and circumstantial resources. These may be gifts from our Lord, but they are different for every one of us, and we are responsible to use them for His glory. We refer to a person as *talented* when he or she has been endowed with outstanding abilities in some field. The expression comes from this very parable.

God has endowed all His servants with certain talents, and He expects us to use these for Him. The five-talented servant was not expected to produce the same result as the two-talented servant. The job of both servants was to use what they were given. Both servants who used their talents were commended with the same blessing: "Well done, good and faithful slave" (vv. 21, 23).

The solemn part of the parable is that the expectations of the master did not allow for the nonproductive servant who hid his talent. Laziness was apparently at the root of his failure, for the master condemned him with the words, "You wicked, lazy slave" (v. 26). Too many servants of God have "hidden" their talents through laziness. May we who serve God be careful to be diligent in using the talents He has entrusted to us. The day of accounting is not far away, and we will be responsible to the Master.

TWELVE

More Than an Apostle—A Servant

If there is a mastermind behind the New Testament strategy of mission, it is Paul. If there is a model for the planting of churches, Paul is that model. If there is a statesman for the early church, no one outshines Paul. He is a leader par excellence. Isn't it remarkable then that Paul, without a trace of false humility, constantly refers to himself as a *servant*.

A Servant's Position

In the first chapter we discussed three Greek words translated "servant." Paul makes use of all of them when describing his own position and work. The first of these is *doulos*, a general word for slave or servant, often translated bond-servant or bondslave. It indicates full subjection to a master. Roman slaves were called *doulos*, and Paul seemed to take delight in using this word to describe his own ministry, particularly in introducing himself in his letters. The Roman letter, for example, begins with, "Paul, a bond-servant of Christ Jesus." Philippians begins with a similar phrase: "Paul and Timothy, bond-servants of Christ Jesus." The letter to Titus also uses the phrase, "Paul, a bond-servant of God." The phrase "ourselves as your bond-servants for Jesus' sake" describes how Paul saw himself and Timothy (2 Cor. 4:5). He linked himself with others in bond-servanthood (Epaphras and Tychicus, for example—Col. 1:7; 4:7).

The verb form of *doulos* is also used of Paul's labors. "Serving the Lord with all humility" was how he put it to the elders of the church at Ephesus (Acts 20:19). And Paul told the Philippians that Timothy "served with me in the furtherance of the gospel" (2:22).

Another word Paul used to describe himself as a "servant" is *diakonos*, a word used for anyone doing service-oriented work, and from which we get the English word *deacon*. The thrust of the word is on the work being done, whereas the emphasis of *doulos* is on submission to the master.

Notice the emphasis on the doing of the work in 1 Corinthians 3, where Paul was protesting party strife in the church:

> For when one says, "I am of Paul," and another, "I am of Apollos," are you not mere men? What then is Apollos? And what is Paul? Servants through whom you believed. (v. 2)

Those who brought the gospel to the Corinthians were merely servants (*diakonos*). It was God's work that the servants were doing, so the Corinthians should align themselves with Him, not with the instruments God used.

Another example of *diakonos* is found in 2 Corinthians 6:4, and here too the emphasis is on the work: "in everything commending ourselves as servants of God, in much endurance . . ." Paul was content to be a servant in the doing of the work of God.

A third word Paul uses for himself as a servant is *litourgos*, which has to do with public and priestly service. For example: "a minister [servant] of Christ Jesus to the Gentiles, ministering [serving] as a priest the gospel of God" (Rom. 15:16).

Paul certainly had learned a lesson in humility—no hypocrisy, no pretending. Paul counted it an honor to be called a servant of God— a *doulos* in subjection to his Master, a *diakonos* doing the work of his Master, and a *litourgos* bringing the gospel to lost people.

A Servant's Character

Paul was not content to be called a servant because of what he did. He wanted to be a servant from the inside out, in his character. In

2 Corinthians he speaks a great deal about his ministry (service), but the work does not stand alone. It is associated with the character of the worker. In chapter 4 there is a good example: "Therefore since we have this ministry, as we received mercy, we do not lose heart . . . not walking in craftiness . . . but by the manifestation of the truth commending ourselves to every man's conscience in the sight of God" (vv. 1-3).

Those whom Paul served would not only hear a sermon, but would see one. His character was consistent with his service. The *Phillips* paraphrase says, "We use no clever tricks, no dishonest manipulation of the Word of God. We speak the plain truth and so commend ourselves to every man's conscience in the sight of God." Paul's love, patience, and gentleness showed that he was a genuine servant. In verse 5 of the same passsage he states, "For we do not preach ourselves but Christ Jesus as Lord, and ourselves as your bond-servants for Jesus' sake." The Corinthians could accept his message as genuine because of the quality of his servant-character.

Paul instructed his disciple Timothy, "And the Lord's bond-servant must not be quarrelsome, but be kind to all, able to teach, patient when wronged, with gentleness correcting those who are in opposition" (2 Tim. 2:24, 25). In describing his ministry to the people of Thessalonica Paul says, "Nor did we seek glory from men . . . even though as apostles of Christ we might have asserted our authority. But we proved to be gentle among you, as a nursing mother tenderly cares for her own children" (1 Thess. 2:6, 7). He treated them with love and tenderness, with their best good in mind, serving them as a mother serves her children.

True servants don't wear masks. They serve well because they are servants. Paul, motivated by the Lord Jesus, displayed true servanthood to the people in Corinth: "For we do not preach ourselves, but Christ Jesus as Lord and ourselves as your bond-servants for Jesus' sake" (2 Cor. 4:5). His servanthood was genuine because the glory of his Lord was its foundation. He could remind the elders at Ephesus, "You yourselves know . . . how I was with you the whole time, serving the Lord with all humility" (Acts 20:18, 19). He wore no mask. His character as servant was genuine.

A Servant's Submission

The Biblical servant freely and voluntarily gives himself to serve both God and man. Paul said, "I have made myself a slave to all, that I might win the more" (1 Cor. 9:19). Submission to the will of his Father was paramount from the moment of his conversion on the Damascus Road. Paul's first words when he heard the voice from Heaven were, "Who art Thou, Lord?" (Acts 9:5). He acknowledged Jesus as Lord. From that moment on, Paul was the servant of the Lord Jesus Christ. If we truly call Jesus Lord, then we must submit to Him in everything.

Paul's next question revealed his submission: "What shall I do, Lord?" (Acts 22:10). Submissive obedience is the attitude of all true servants, the first step of discipleship, and Paul willingly took it.

Paul's submission was not that of a cowering slave working in fear of the master's whip. There is dignity in the service of the Lord Jesus Christ, a dignity which comes from pleasing the Master and accomplishing His purposes. Even while Paul was prostrate in the dust of the Damascus Road, the Lord gave him a special assignment: "Arise, and stand on your feet; for this purpose I have appeared to you, to appoint you a minister" (Acts 26:16). The Greek word translated "minister" here comes from the imagery of ancient ships manned by dozens of oarsmen—slaves. They had no choice in where they were going and no knowledge of what dangers lay ahead. Rowing to the captain's beat—complete submission to the captain— was all that mattered.

Paul counted it an honor to be a slave of Christ for the progress of world evangelism (see 1 Cor. 4:1)—"to open their eyes that they may turn from darkness to light and from the dominion of Satan to God" (Acts 26:18). With a purpose like that in view, his choice to be a servant of Christ makes perfect sense.

Paul's voluntary submission was manward as well as Godward, making himself a servant to men for the sake of the gospel, a debtor to all, paying his obligation by sharing the Good News with them. To the Corinthians he said, "I have made myself a slave to all, that I might win the more" (1 Cor. 9:19). He submitted himself to the Lord as one sent with the gospel; he submitted himself to man to bring them the gospel (Col. 1:23).

Paul taught servanthood to others as well. The Roman believers were instructed that in light of all the mercies of God, they were to present their bodies as "a living and holy sacrifice, acceptable to God" (Rom. 12:1). Paul called this act of submission their "reasonable service" (KJV) or their "spiritual service of worship." Paul used the same word in the first chapter when he said, "For God, whom I serve in my spirit in the preaching of the gospel of His Son . . ." (Rom. 1:9). What Paul did, the Romans were to do. Their service, beginning with submission at the altar as a living sacrifice, was commitment to the Lordship of Christ.

A Servant's Task
Submission is a first-cousin of obedience. Speaking the first time he met the Lord, Paul testified, "Consequently, King Agrippa, I did not prove disobedient to the heavenly vision" (Acts 26:19). When Paul understood the mind of God, he obeyed and put it into action.

Sometimes Paul had specific guidance from God—the vision of the man from Macedonia, for example: "we sought to go into Macedonia, concluding that God had called us to preach the gospel to them" (Acts 16:10). More often Paul's obedience was general in nature. He knew that his commission was to preach the gospel, so he obeyed by seeking every opportunity to do that. He was striving to do everything to the glory of the Lord Jesus Christ, to accomplish the purposes of God as he understood them.

A Servant's Message
Serving God, for Paul, was linked with gospel outreach. To the Colossians he spoke of "the gospel . . . of which I Paul was made a minister [servant]" (Col. 1:23). To the Ephesians he said, "I was made a minister [servant] . . . to preach to the Gentiles the unfathomable riches of Christ" (Eph. 3:7, 8). And to the Romans he wrote, "for God whom I serve in my spirit in the preaching of the gospel of His Son . . ." (Rom. 1:9).

He describes his gospel preaching as "the ministry [service] of reconciliation" (2 Cor. 5:18). The greatest service that Paul could render to people outside of Christ was to bring them the message of reconciliation. He had been appointed a minister to both Jew and

Gentile, "to open their eyes so that they may turn from darkness to light and from the dominion of Satan to God in order that they may receive forgiveness of sins" (Acts 26:18). Those of us who are servants of God need a heart like Paul's, aflame with a passion for the souls of men.

A Servant's Work

Paul loved the people of God and gave himself in service to them. When he says, "Of this church I was made a minister" (Col. 1:25) he was not speaking of ordination or position. He was saying that he was made a servant to the family of God, to assist them, to encourage them. Like the Lord Jesus, he wanted to serve, not be served.

Seeing himself and his co-workers as "your bond-servants for Jesus' sake" (2 Cor. 4:5), he was willing to go to any lengths, to bear any burden for them which would glorify the Lord Jesus. No job was too hard or too demeaning. The Corinthians were "cared for" by him (2 Cor. 3:3). He nurtured the Thessalonian believers "as a nursing mother tenderly cares for her own children" (1 Thess. 2:7). "I will most gladly spend and be expended for your souls" (2 Cor. 12:15)—that's servanthood!

A Servant's Suffering

One of the uncomfortable realities about Biblical servanthood is that it involves suffering. The Lord Jesus suffered as a servant, and those who would be like Him will also. To the Philippians Paul wrote, "For to you it has been granted for Christ's sake, not only to believe in Him, but also to suffer for His sake" (1:29). Paul himself was no exception. From the moment of his conversion, suffering became the pattern of his life. One of the first things the Lord revealed to the disciple Ananias about Paul was that he would suffer many things for the Lord (Acts 9:16), even though he escaped over the wall of Damascus in a basket. Practically everything that he formerly valued he lost, because Christ was now his first priority. "For [Him]," he said, "I have suffered the loss of all things, and count them but rubbish" (Phil. 3:8).

Paul was the guardian of a sacred trust, the gospel. In fulfilling his responsibility to keep it safe in a hostile world, suffering was inevitable. "After we had already suffered and been mistreated in

Philippi, as you know, we had the boldness in our God to speak to you the gospel of God amid much opposition . . . just as we have been approved by God to be entrusted with the gospel, so we speak, not as pleasing men but God" (1 Thess. 2:2-4).

In addition to suffering for the gospel, Paul suffered for the sake of the church. The church in Corinth is an example: "The sufferings of Christ are ours in abundance. . . . But if we are afflicted, it is for your comfort and salvation" (2 Cor. 1:5, 6). Servanthood in the church often brings trials.

> . . . but in everything commending ourselves as servants of God, in much endurance, in afflictions, in hardships, in distresses, in beatings, in imprisonments, in tumults, in labors, in sleeplessness, in hunger, in purity, in knowledge, in patience, in kindness, in the Holy Spirit, in genuine love, . . . by glory and dishonor, by evil reports and good report . . . as unknown yet well-known. . . . Our mouth has spoken freely to you, O Corinthians, our heart is opened wide. (2 Cor. 6:4-11)

All this Paul gladly endured as a servant of Christ. Later in the letter he reminded them that he had suffered far more than the false teachers who claimed to be servants of God, but in fact had avoided suffering. "Are they servants of Christ?" he challenged; "I more so; in far more labors, in far more imprisonments . . ." (2 Cor. 11:23).

For Paul the path to glory was a path of suffering. "We suffer with Him [Christ] in order that we may also be glorified with Him. For I consider that the sufferings of this present time are not worthy to be compared with the glory that is to be revealed to us" (Rom. 8:17, 18). What he suffered of Christ, he considered as sharing in the sufferings of Christ, "the fellowship of His sufferings" (Phil. 3:10). To the Colossians he said, "Now I rejoice in my sufferings for your sake" (Col. 1:24). How like the Lord, who came to serve and to give His life a ransom for many.

We would do well to follow the example Paul left us. He was never ashamed to be a servant. At the height of a storm, when the seamen had lost all hope of survival, Paul told them, "An angel of the God to whom I belong and whom I serve stood before me . . ." (Acts 27:24). That was the story of his life. He belonged to God as a bondservant, and he delighted to serve Him.

THIRTEEN

At the Feet of Jesus

God gives us some fascinating thumbnail sketches of New Testament characters whose service provides models for us. From these we will gain valuable insights into serving God more effectively.

Stephanas:
The Commitment of Serving

One of the little-known men of the New Testament is Stephanas (almost the same name as the famous Stephen who was a leader in the early church and became the first martyr; both names mean crown or crowned). Stephanas is only mentioned at the beginning and end of 1 Corinthians: Paul had baptized Stephanas and his household (1:16); Stephanas was evidently the first to be converted in Corinth (16:15). As one of the leaders of the Corinthian church, he was chosen with two others to take a financial gift from Corinth to Paul in Ephesus (see 16:17). Along with the gift was a letter, Paul's answer to which we call 1 Corinthians. Stephanas and his companions evidently took that letter back with them to Corinth.

Paul makes a significant comment about Stephanas and his household: "You know the household of Stephanas, that they were the firstfruits of Achaia, and that they have devoted themselves for ministry to the saints" (16:15). "Devoted" means they had "set themselves" for the task; this carries the idea of commitment. Stephanas was committed to serving the people of God, and the next verse adds that he "help[ed] in the work."

Our churches are packed with people who want to be fed and entertained, to have their needs met. Where are the people who will wholeheartedly devote themselves to serving others as a first priority?

Because of Stephanas' commitment to service in the church, Paul urged the Corinthians to be "in subjection to such men" (16:16) and to "acknowledge such men" (16:18). It is easy to trust a leader who has demonstrated sensitivity and caring through service to others. Would to God that our local churches were full of leaders like Stephanas.

Archippus:
The Source of Serving

Archippus, mentioned only twice in the Bible, lived in Colosse, a city in what is today western Turkey. Paul's letter to Philemon, a prominent man in Colosse, mentions Archippus as a "fellow-soldier" (Philem. 2), one of Paul's favorite terms for those who had fought along with him in the battle for men's souls. Evidently people had been snatched from the hands of the Enemy as Archippus fought as a good soldier of Jesus Christ.

The second mention of Archippus gives us insight into serving. When Paul wrote to the Colossian believers from his Roman prison, he mentioned a number of Christians by name. Right at the end he had a special word of exhortation for Archippus: "And say to Archippus, 'Take heed to the ministry which you have received in the Lord, that you may fulfill it' " (4:17). The source of Archippus' ministry (service) was the Lord; God had given him a job to do. The point was that the job description and the appointment came from God Himself.

Phillips puts it plainly: "Remember that the Lord ordained you to your ministry—see that you carry it out." Knowing that the living God has appointed us gives us a mighty incentive to "tough it out." Archippus may have been slacking off, or at least was in danger of doing so. Paul's message to him was that if he drew back from his ministry, he would be letting God down. Neither he nor we can afford to let up.

Martha:
The Purpose of Serving
Martha of Bethany, perhaps one of the best-known servants in the New Testament, is often seen in contrast to her sister Mary, who sat at the feet of the Lord Jesus while Martha was busy in the kitchen. It is true that Mary's deep longing to know the Lord and her humility in learning at His feet is the Christian's highest priority, and Martha needed to learn that. The Lord pointed out that such worship is the one thing which is really necessary (Luke 10:38-42).

Martha was serving, but in the hectic rush she forgot the real purpose of it. Luke tells us that she was "distracted with all her preparations" (v. 40). It bothered her that Mary was not helping and that the Lord didn't seem to have noticed this. She complained, "Lord, do You not care that my sister has left me to do all the serving alone? Then tell her to help me" (v. 40).

There was nothing wrong with her service, but its object had become distorted. The Lord gently rebuked her for her excessive attention to material provisions. She had wanted to be noticed; she wanted the Lord to tell Mary to help her in the kitchen. She had lost the attitude of a real servant.

But the Biblical record does not leave the story of Martha there. John completes it in his Gospel (11:1—12:2). He shows us that Martha had learned the lesson well, for she shined as a woman of great faith when her brother Lazarus died. She gave one of the outstanding testimonies in all of Scripture as to who Christ was (11:27). After talking to the Lord, she went to call Mary (v. 28). No jealousy here. Moments later, though she did not at first think that Lazarus would be raised, she had the stone removed from his grave, and so saw "the glory of God" as the Lord promised her (vv. 39-41).

The next time Jesus visited Bethany (12:2) Martha was serving as usual, Mary was back at His feet, Lazarus was reclining at table with the Lord. But there was not even a whisper of a complaint from Martha. Now it was service with a smile instead of with a grumble. Why the change? "They made Him a supper; and Martha was serving" (12:2). Her purpose was to serve *Him*. No longer did it matter how much work she did or who was (or wasn't) helping. The purpose she had before her made all the difference.

When Martha's purpose was to demonstate her prowess as a

homemaker and cook, she became easily distracted and frustrated. When her purpose was to please the Lord, to make a supper for Him, then she could continue without complaint. The primary lesson in serving is crucial for us today.

Phoebe:
The Help of Service

There is a fascinating little note in the last chapter of Romans about another Christian woman who served with excellence (Rom. 16:1, 2). Phoebe's name means "bright, radiant, or pure." Phoebe was a Christian woman living in Cenchrea, one of the port cities of Corinth, which, located on a narrow isthmus between the Aegean and the Adriatic Seas, had a port on each side. Paul had visited there (Acts 18:18) and a church had been planted, although we have no record of the details.

In writing the letter to the Romans while in Corinth, Paul learned that Phoebe planned to travel to Rome. In all likelihood, she took the letter to the Roman believers. That letter is the doctrinal heart of the New Testament, and Phoebe had the privilege of serving the Roman church by bringing it to them.

Paul encouraged the Romans to receive Phoebe as a sister into the fellowship of the local church there: "I commend to you our sister Phoebe . . . receive her in the Lord in a manner worthy of the saints" (16:1, 2). He was introducing her as a person worthy of their Christian fellowship and asked them to help her in any way needed.

Paul called Phoebe "a servant of the church" (v. 1). She was to be helped because she herself had helped many and Paul too (v. 2). Probably a woman of some wealth, Phoebe stands as an example of godly service to the church. While today women's "rights" are a crucial issue in many churches and more authority for women is being demanded, Phoebe gladly took the servant role and gladly helped others.

Onesimus:
The Usefulness of Service

Onesimus was a slave of Philemon of Colosse. He stole some money from his master and ran away, and eventually found himself in Rome where he ran into the Apostle Paul. Converted to Christ, Onesimus faced now the moral question of his responsibility for his past misdeeds. (A runaway slave would normally be killed if caught.) An interesting complication existed in that the master of Onesimus, Philemon, was a Christian whom Paul knew.

The right thing was for the lawful slave of Philemon to go back. Paul loved Onesimus, who had endeared himself to the apostle by serving him in prison; so Paul wrote a letter to Philemon and sent it with Onesimus. In the letter he explained the situation and pleaded for Philemon to forgive Onesimus, even offering to pay any financial demands himself. If Philemon loved and respected Paul, which he did, there was no way he could refuse the aged missionary. As far as we know, Philemon did forgive his errant slave.

Paul's commendation of Onesimus as a servant is interesting: "I appeal to you for my child, whom I have begotten in my imprisonment, Onesimus, who formerly was useless to you, but now is useful both to you and to me" (Philem. 10, 11). There is a play on words here connected with the name Onesimus, which means "useful." As a thief and a runaway, he was useless; as a believer he had become like his name, useful. Isn't that what servants are for, to be useful?

Evidently Onesimus had been serving Paul in some meaningful way. Perhaps he was preparing food, or carrying messages from Paul to others in Rome. Whatever it was, Paul says of him, "I have sent him back to you in person, that is, sending my very heart; whom I wished to keep with me, that in your behalf he might minister to [serve] me in my imprisonment for the gospel" (vv. 12, 13). As servants of Christ and one another we find our usefulness.

Paul:
The Selflessness of Serving
The second chapter of Philippians is one of the outstanding passages of Scripture dealing with servanthood. It begins with an exhortation to have a servant attitude—personal interests are not to take precedence over the interests of others (vv. 3, 4). The ultimate example is the Lord Jesus Christ: "Have this attitude in yourselves which was also in Christ Jesus, who . . . taking the form of a bond-servant . . . humbled Himself by becoming obedient to the point of death, even death on a cross" (vv. 5-8).

The remainder of the chapter gives three human examples of servanthood: Paul, Timothy, and Epaphroditus. Paul says of himself, "But even if I am being poured out as a drink offering upon the sacrifice and service of your faith, I rejoice and share my joy with you all" (v. 17). Paul compares himself to the "drink offering" of the Old Testament (Num. 15:1-12). In connection with the burnt offering, wine was ceremonially poured out on the sacrificial lamb as it was placed upon the altar, picturing the Lord Jesus Christ who "poured out Himself to death" (Isa. 53:12). The wine poured onto the offering was immediately lost to view.

This is the imagery Paul used. Paul was happy to be an unnoticed part of what the Philippians were doing for God. What an example of humility in service! Such an attitude resembles the Lord Jesus Himself who "made Himself of no reputation" or "emptied Himself" (Phil. 2:7). Too few Christians who think of themselves as servants of God are willing to be a drink offering on the service of others. We become jealous of their ministry and envious of their successes. But if we are really servants, we will rejoice whenever our Lord is glorified.

Timothy:
The Excellence of Serving

Another example of servanthood in Philippians 2 is Timothy (vv. 18-24). It is interesting that Paul, who only mentions himself in one verse in this passage, has much more to say of the service of both Timothy and Epaphroditus in the following verses. Timothy is held up as one who "served with me in the furtherance of the gospel" (v. 22). The excellence of his service was this: "I have no one else of kindred spirit who will be genuinely concerned for your welfare" (v. 20).

Unlike so many others, Timothy's interest in the Philippians was genuine. There were no mixed motives, no selfish desires. Timothy was like a child serving his father, obedient and faithful (v. 22). Others "seek their own interests, not those of Christ Jesus" (v. 21), but Timothy was different. He would be concerned for their welfare, even at the expense of his own. He was willing to serve and willing to go when and where he was sent.

Epaphroditus:
The Limits of Serving

The final example of servanthood in Philippians 2 is Epaphroditus, who had recently come from Philippi to Rome where Paul was in prison. He had brought with him an offering (money) from the believers, and Paul calls him "your messenger and minister to my need" (v. 25). It was a long way from Philippi to Rome, but Epaphroditus had made the journey to assure Paul of the love of the Philippian church. Having arrived in Rome, he had become very sick for an extended period of time. News of his illness had reached Philippi, so the Philippians had written to express their concern. Now Paul is writing to them and pays some remarkable compliments to Epaphroditus.

Paul describes him as "my brother" (v. 25), indicating their commonality in the family of faith. He is called a "fellow-worker" of Paul's and a "fellow-soldier" too, indicating his willingness to be involved in the battle. Paul concludes his list of compliments by calling him "your messenger and minister to my need."

Epaphroditus loved the people back home and was anxious to get back to service there. He was concerned that they were worried by his sickness and was more concerned for their well-being than for his own (v. 26). Paul wrote to encourage the Philippians to give him a hero's welcome when he arrived home. Why? "Because he came close to death for the work of Christ, risking his life to complete what was deficient in your service to me" (v. 30). Epaphroditus was willing to risk his life for others. Willingness to go all the way was what marked this servant. There was no task too difficult, no place too far away, no price too costly.

One of the things that characterizes Christians today is a low degree of commitment. People fail to show up because the weather is not what they expected. They drop out of a ministry because it interferes with a bowling night. They resign because another won't cooperate. Excuse after excuse pours out, but the real reason for their failure is that the limits of service are fixed by self-interest. Epaphroditus provides us with an example of true Christian service. The presenting of our body as a living sacrifice is, after all, our reasonable service (Rom. 12:1). Sacrifices do not put limits on the fire.

Tychicus:
The Obedience of Serving

One of the outstanding servant-characters of the New Testament is Tychicus, mentioned in five books. Paul counted him among his most trusted co-workers. Small wonder, for Tychicus was everything a servant should be—trustworthy, faithful, willing, loyal, obedient.

During his third missionary journey, Paul collected money from churches in all of the areas of his missionary outreach to help the poor Christians in Jerusalem. Each collection area selected trustworthy men to take the money with Paul to Jerusalem, and Tychicus was one man chosen from the churches in Asia (Acts 20:4). He was happy to give himself to this task for the believers and for the glory of God.

Tychicus is next seen three years later in Rome during Paul's first imprisonment. Paul writes about the special service of this man in two letters (Eph. 6:21, 22; Col. 4:7, 8). The description of him in both is revealing. He was a "beloved brother and faithful servant and fellow-bondslave." First, he is an equal in the family of God. Paul and Tychicus were brothers; they loved and respected each other.

The second relationship between these two men was master/servant. Tychicus was happy to take a humble role of obedience to the leadership of the older apostle. A "faithful servant," he played second fiddle.

> It takes more grace than I can tell
> To play the second fiddle well.

Tychicus understood that faithful followers are true servants.

His third relationship to Paul was as "fellow-bondslave." Both regarded themselves as bond-servants of the Lord Jesus Christ. Bought with a price, redeemed from the slavemarket of sin, they gladly submitted themselves to their new Master as slaves of His grace.

The references in Ephesians and Colossians indicate another assignment Tychicus received from Paul: to carry both letters from Rome to the two cities, along with a personal letter to Philemon. The manuscripts for three New Testament books were placed in his care over a long and difficult journey. He was a trustworthy servant.

Two more assignments of Tychicus are noted in the New Testament. When writing to Titus in Crete, Paul tells him that Tychicus is available to be sent to replace him so Titus could visit Paul in Nicopolis between his two Roman imprisonments (3:12). Again Tychicus is an obedient servant.

The final look at Tychicus in the Bible (2 Tim. 4:12) mentions that Tychicus has been sent to Ephesus. Right to the last he fulfills the role of the servant to Paul, going where he is sent, doing what he is instructed to do. Obedience was the hallmark of his servanthood.

Onesiphorus:
The Courage of Serving

Two brief references in Paul's final book tell us all we know about Onesiphorus (2 Tim. 1:16-18; 4:19). Apparently a resident of Ephesus, during Paul's imprisonment he had occasion to visit Rome and while there sought out the apostle. Paul says he "eagerly searched for me" (1:17). When he had found Paul, Onesiphorus often "refreshed" him (1:16), meaning that he provided friendship and probably financial help as well. Paul commended him for his "services" while still in Ephesus also (1:18). These no doubt were in the context of the church there. All churches need people who want to serve.

The thing that stands out in particular about the service of Onesiphorus is his courage. Paul recalls him in contrast to two men, Phygelus and Hermogenes, who had become ashamed of Paul as a prisoner and had turned away from him (1:15). Their rejection disappointed the aged apostle, but he obtained great comfort from the courage of Onesiphorus, who "was not ashamed of my chains" and remained faithful (1:16). The stigma of a court case and imprisonment made no difference to Onesiphorus. Accepting personal risk, he found the condemned apostle and ministered to him. What an example of courage in service.

Conclusion

The Scripture clearly teaches us that the person God uses has the heart of a servant. The central focus of our servanthood is the Lord Jesus Christ, the perfect Servant who has become our Master. A poem was found in the Bible of J. N. Darby which beautifully states the relationship between the Lord Jesus and His servants.

> Low at Thy Feet, Lord Jesus,
> This is the place for me,
> Here I have learned deep lessons,
> Truth that has set me free.
>
> Free from myself, Lord Jesus,
> Free from the ways of men,
> Chains of thought that have bound me
> Never can bind again.
>
> None but Thyself, Lord Jesus,
> Conquered this wayward will,
> But for Thy love constraining
> I had been wayward still.

Submission to Him is demonstrated by submission to one another. A cup of cold water given in His name to a fellow-human is an act of service to Him (Matt. 25:34-40). The command to "through love serve one another" (Gal. 5:13) leaves us no option. A local church which abounds in servants, from the leaders to the least, will be a healthy, happy, growing church.

Serving the Lord with gladness is service (ministry) based on love, His love.

> I gave my service but with a heavy heart,
> And with it went but little love or trust,
> He was my Master, I must serve,
> And so I gave my service, for I must.
>
> Then o'er the dreary dullness of my road
> There came the kindling ray of better thought,
> I owed my service to a loving God,
> And so I gave my service, for I ought.
>
> And lo, the Master made the service sweet,
> And like a ray of glory from above
> There came the knowledge that to serve was joy,
> And so I gave my service, for I love.

Scripture Index